CAPPADOCIA

Turgay Tuna
Bülent Demirdurak

CAPPADOCIA

GUIDE

Contents

Introduction

The region of Cappadocia resembles another planet, one that is transformed from one color to another every season of the year, every hour of the day. Basalt rock, covered in tuff by spewing volcanoes thousands of years ago, and mystical fairy chimneys make one wonder where exactly one is. It is impossible to be unaffected by the enchanting mystery of this incomparable natural wonder.

In this book you will find detailed information that has been prepared for your travels to what is perhaps Turkey's most mystical region. Authors Turgay Tuna and Bülent Demirdurak have combined their knowledge and experience to guide you to enjoyable excursions in this region. Writer, tourist guide and world-traveller Turgay Tuna spends half his year in Cappadocia. Bülent Demirdurak has fulfilled his childhood dream for the past 40 years by travelling and guiding tourists, and is also a travel writer. Both men are knowledgable about every detail of Cappadocia, from its history to its fauna, from its most hidden corners to its most widely known wonders, and both have published many articles and books on this subject.

Another writer-photographer who cherishes the region, the director of Nevşehir Museum, Murat Gülyaz has kindly permitted us to use some of the most beautiful photographs he has taken of the region; he even ventured into the field in the summer heat to take photographs especially for us. Gülyaz, in addition, has updated the book in line with the recent findings and information, integrated missing information and corrected unnoticed mistakes.

What is there to see in Cappadocia, how do you get there and what can you do? The region is a paradise for those who enjoy discovering variety and contrast. In excursions to the valleys adorned with fairy chimneys you can discover places that have never been visited before, and if you are interested in photography you will be able to take extremely diverse pictures. You can hike, ride horseback, enjoy an incredible hot-air balloon ride, and even observe a demonstration of *sema*, the whirling of dervishes. You can visit the valleys and underground cities, you can ride a bicycle.

Even if you've been there many times, every trip to Cappadocia will hold a surprise, and you can visit during every season of the year. Sometimes the fairy chimneys will appear before you covered with snow, sometimes adorned with wildflowers. If you are devoted to winter sports, Mount Erciyes and its ski center, only 45 minutes away, can provide you with the best possible opportunity to satisfy your indulgence.

You can visit Cappadocia for three days, but bear in mind that you may want to remain there for weeks! Where to start and where to finish your excursion is up to you. For a typical three-day tour, the first day could start with a trip to the underground cities of Kaymaklı or Derinkuyu, continue to the Uçhisar Güvercinlik [dovecote] area to take photographs, and on to Avcılar. At around 11:30 proceed to the Göreme Valley to visit the churches, particularly those of Karanlık and Tokalı, and after lunch go on to the Paşabağ and Zelve valleys. To view the sunset, return to the Uçhisar Fortress. On the second day, start by visiting Ortahisar and its fortress before continuing to the Soğanlı Valley, stopping along the way at Mustafapaşa, and continuing at day's end to Ürgüp and Avanos. You can dedicate the third day to Güzelyurt, Ihlara and Belisırma.

As a convenience to the visitors, locations on the approximately same route are covered together. A short glossary in the back of the book will be your indispensable helper in deciphering the stories in the church frescoes.

Editor

Pages 8-9, scene from Çavuşin.

Below, the Nativity, Karanlık Church, Göreme.

HISTORY AND CULTURE

Distinctive topography

Cappadocia, a region of volcanic tuff, basalt and andesite rock, was in antiquity bordered on the north by the lands of Pontus, to the west by Phrygia, whose boundaries were delineated by the Halys River (Kızılırmak) and Lake Tatta (Tuz Gölü), to the southeast by the nation of Kommagenes, circumscribed by the Euphrates (Fırat) River, and to the south by the lands of Cilicia. The region known as Cappadocia then included the present-day provinces of Çorum, Yozgat, Sivas, Malatya, Kayseri, Nevşehir, Kırşehir and Niğde, together with parts of the provinces of Tokat, Kahramanmaraş, Adana and Konya. Today's Cappadocia is a region of approximately 300 km² covered by the provinces Nevşehir, Aksaray, Niğde, Kayseri and Kırşehir.

The evolution of the region has been taking place for 60,000,000 years. During the Third Geological Era the Taurus Mountains were formed, and under pressure from the Anatolian plateau to the north, large and small volcanoes became active, with the lava flow erupting from Mount Hasan to the south, and Göllüdağ and an assortment of other large and small volcanoes in the middle, vast plateaus were covered by the accumulated ash, eventually forming a soft layer of tuff. Contrary to general belief, Mount Erciyes has had no effect on the formation of fairy chimneys and the central rocky Cappadocia since this volcano is much younger than the others. When the volcanic activity ceased, erosion began to abrade the softer soil and the harder stone began to emerge. During this long process, in some areas layers of up to 100 meters of tuff were covered by occasional deposits of lava composed of hard basalt.

Over thousands of years, rainwater draining through cracks began to wear away the soft layers of tuff, while the winds, along with warming and cooling air, assisted the erosion. It was in this manner that cones embedded in mushroom-like shapes eventually formed on the tops of hills that were not affected by the erosion. Today these formations that we observe with such admiration have been named 'fairy chimneys'. The layers of tuff that were not covered with basalt were subject to formation through erosion and were transformed into the valleys that extend one after the other, and eventually into canyons, one more beautiful than the other.

The layerings of tuff are what give the fairy chimneys and canyons of Cappadocia their legendary beauty, and

Pages 14-15, a Cappadocian panaroma from Uçhisar.

Opposite page, fairy chimneys with caps offer unique scenes throughout Cappadocia.

because of the ease with which the stone is worked, it became the primary material for architectural works that were created by carving the stone. Numerous churches, monasteries and homes were carved from this stone. And because the tuff does not absorb paint, the unique frescoes adorning the rock churches can still be seen today.

Opposite page, picture of a horse which shows the influence of the local art of Cappadocia, which is famous for its quality horses. Karşı Church, Gülşehir.

Below, terracotta goddess statuette found in Köşkhöyük. 6000 BC., Niğde Museum.

Lowermost, Zankhöyük, west of Avanos, near Sarılar Village.

History of the country of beautiful horses

The first presence of man in Cappadocia occurred in the Lower Paleolithic period, approximately 500.000 years ago. Tools made of silex and obsidian dating from this period have been discovered in Suvermez near Derinkuyu and Soğanlı Valley within the province of Kayseri. Discoveries in archaeological excavations testify to human presence at Çatalhöyük in 10,000-9,000 BC and at Aşıklıhöyük, near the Ihlara Valley, in 10,000 BC. In the Civelek Cave, remains from the Calcolitic Period have been identified. Mother goddess sculptures, jewelry and painted pottery discovered at the mounds provide clear and important information regarding the regional culture's past. These discoveries are exhibited at Nevşehir Museum.

Kitchen utensils, clay vessels and other discoveries made in 1991 during the excavation of Zankhöyük, located 20 km north of Avanos, have been dated to the Bronze Age (3.000-1200 BC). Proto-Hittite and Hittite activity in the region continued until the 1200s BC. It is generally accepted that the years of Anatolian occupation coincide with the end of the Hittite era. Because of its geographic situation, throughout history this area was unable to defend itself against external invasion, and consequently it was impossible to establish large settlements.

During the beginning of the sixth century BC Cappadocia was invaded by the Medes. After 547 BC the Persians, having brought the region under their dominion, constituted a major power. Cappodocia became one of the thirty-one satraps, or provinces with an appointed governor, that the Persians established in Anatolia. The Persians collected an annual tax consisting of 1,500 horses, 2,000 cattle and 20,000 sheep from their Cappadocia satrap. It was during this era that Cappadocia was named Katpa-

Above right, coin of
the Cappadocian king,
Ariarathes IV.

Below right, coin of
Caesarea.

toukia or Katpatuka. Although 'country of beautiful horses' in
the Persian language is Huv-aspa literally, Katpatuka was the
name associated with the places where quality horses were found.

The Macedonians who arrived in 333 BC with Alexander the Great became the new power in Anatolia. While
Alexander the Great was moving on to Cilicia, Ariarathes
I became the king of Cappadocia. During the short period
thereafter, the boundaries of the Kingdom of Cappadocia extended from the Euphrates River to the shores of the Black
Sea. After the early demise of Alexander the Great, who died
without an heir apparent, the struggles that began among his
generals continued unceasingly for three hundred years.

After the death of Ariarathes I, the throne passed to
Ariarathes II, and the boundaries of the Kingdom of Cappadocia continued to expand. During the reign of Ariarathes
V artists and men of learning were highly esteemed; but after
this sovereign's death, the region changed hands several times
between the Romans and the Pontic kings.

In 47 BC, Julius Caesar settled his army into the area
around Mazaka. After the victory over the Pontic king, the
name of Mazaka was changed to Caesarea, today's Kayseri.
The Hellenistic Era ended in 30 BC, and Cappadocia became
the seventeenth province of Rome.

After the year 310, strife began to break out throughout
the Roman Empire. In 312 the Emperor Constantine divided
the empire into East and West and accepted Christianity as his

religion, although to what extent Christian is a matter for discussion. Constantine was baptized in 337, on his deathbed. Making peace with the church in 313, Constantine recognized freedom of conscience and liberty for all other religions. This incident marked a brand new beginning from the aspect of relations between the church and society. The church would become integrated with all the states who embraced Christianity, ensuring for itself both material and legal advantages. In 324 Constantine defeated his rival in the East, Licinius, thereby becoming the sole administrator of the Empire. On 11 May 330 he established the city of Constantinopolis, named for himself. It was during this period that the important Cappadocian saints, such as Basileios the Great of Caesarea (Kayseri), Gregory of Nazianzos (Nenezi) and Gregory of Nyssa (Nevşehir), began to appear, one by one.

During the reign of the Emperor Valens, in the years 371-372, for reasons of religion, administration and finance, Cappadocia was divided into First Cappadocia and Second Cappadocia. The First Cappadocia capital of Caesarea contained six *diocese*, or cities, while the Second Cappadocia capital Tyana (Kemerhisar) also consisted of six *diocese*. During the reign of the Emperor Justinian, another region, whose capital was Makissos (Kırşehir) and consisted of five *diocese*, was named Third Cappadocia. Between the sixth and ninth centuries the region, which was beginning to become prominent, was connected to the center of the bishopric. In 395, Theodosius the Great, who had succeeded Valentinianus as emperor, died. The Western Roman Empire would collapse after 493 under the explosion of barbarian invasions. In contrast to this, Eastern Rome, whose capital was Constantinopolis, would manage to remain on its feet.

In the vicinity of Tyana (Kemerhisar), aquaduct of Roman Empire Era which brings water from Köşk Pınar known at present as Roman Pool.

During the reign of Emperor Justinianus the Great, between 527 and 567, the golden age of Byzantium began. In the sixth and seventh centuries the first mural paintings–these paintings are incorrectly named as frescoes as fresco is a different painting technique; however, as the term is widespread we will continue to use it as well–were being painted on the walls of the Church of St. John the Baptist in Çavuşin and in the Balkan Deresi and Güllüdere churches in Zelve in Cappadocia. During the seventh and eighth centuries Byzantium began to experience great difficulties as a result of the invasions of Avars, Slavs, Sassanians and Arabs. In addition, internal unrest and the movement of Iconoclasm, which condemned the use of religious imagery and icons, had intensified. The frescoes of the Kızılçukur, Meskendir and Güllüdere churches date to this period.

Between 605 and 611 the Sassanians occupied Kayseri, Syria and Egypt. In 647 Kayseri was overcome by Arab armies, and in 717-718 the Caliph Omar succeeded in advancing into the interior of Anatolia.

Between the years 726 and 780, the period of Iconoclasm began with the reign of Emperor Leo III. The church frescoes, mosaics and icons that explained religion to the people by depicting scenes from the Holy Bible were demolished. Although Iconoclasm was purported to prevent the human figure from interfering between God and man, its true purpose was to destroy the power of the church and the monasteries. Between 746 and 843, the monks who inhabited monasteries were forced

Opposite page, ornaments made by brick-red dyes on the walls of the Church of Saint Barbara, Göreme.

Below, Church of Tokalı II (New Tokalı), Göreme.

to abandon their sanctuaries. Byzantium experienced its second golden age between the ninth and twelfth centuries. It was during this period that domed churches in the form of a Greek cross began to proliferate in Cappadocia, as in Constantinopolis and Anatolia in general. It was during this period, which extended from 867 until 1056, that the era of the Macedonian dynasty began in Byzantium. After his victory in Cilicia, the Emperor Nicophoras Phocas visited Cappadocia, and following his visit the churches began to be decorated with new frescoes, one more beautiful than the other. The churches of Belisırma-

Döner Kümbet, Kayseri.

Direkli, Gülşehir-Aziz Iohannes [St. John], Ortahisar-Tavşanlı and Göreme-Yeni Tokalı belong to this period. The years between 976 and 1025 mark the rise of Byzantium, beginning with the reign of Emperor Basileios II. It was during the years between 1000 and 1075 that the typical Byzantine frescoes that are specific to the region began to appear in Cappadocia.

The Seljuk Turks coming from the Central Asia entered into the Eastern Anatolian lands in the eleventh century. Having defeated the Byzantine army which was commanded by Romenos Diogenes in 1071 in the Plain of Malazgirt, they started to move on towards the central Anatolia. The city of Konya (Iconium) of Byzantine became the capital of Anatolian Seljuk Empire. As in 1082, Kayseri and the other cities of Cappadocia were seized by the Seljuks, Christian Anatolia became to adopt the Islamic religion gradually. Seljukian sultans pursued their policy and sovereignty with great tolerance without any discrimination by religion, language or race. In 1308, Ilkhanids, a branch of the Mogol Empire from the Central Asia, invaded the Seljukian towns. Following the invasion, the Seljuk Empire became ruined and small beyliks emerged in Anatolia. In 1204 the armies of the Fourth Crusade occupied Constantinopolis, and a period of pillage and plunder began. While these events were taking place during the thirteenth century, the art of Cappadocia also began a slow decline that would be followed by gradual disappearance.

Following the dispersion of the Seljuks, the Ottomans started to seize the Western Anatolian lands which were under the dominion of Byzantine Empire. After Bursa and Edirne, the conquest of Constantinopolis in 1453 resulted in the demolish of a 1000-year-empire of Byzantine. One of the most important settlements of Cappadocia, old Nyssa, or Muşkara village as known in Ottomans, was the birthplace of famous vizier Damat İbrahim Paşa. During his service, Muşkara became Nevşehir, which means "new town" in Turkish. Along with Nevşehir, the Cappadocian region started to be embellished by Ottoman structures.

Like in the Seljukian period, during the Ottoman rule as well there was no interference with the faith of the Christians, but the concept of art that had developed in the carved churches was gone, never to return. The signature of the Treaty of Lausanne in 1924 was followed by massive emigration, and unfortunately in the wake of the population exchange practically no Christians were left in the region.

Monastery life in the sheltered valleys

After Jesus was crucified, his apostles spread out to different regions and Christianity entered a new phase. During the Byzantine era numerous churches, monasteries and underground cities were constructed throughout Cappadocia. From the third century onwards there was a significant increase in the Christian population.

When the persecution of Christians began to increase in the fourth century, the shelters carved into the rocks of Cappadocia became a magnet for believers. Later, with the presence of men of religion who would come to be known as the 'Cappadocian Fathers', each of whom would be elevated to sainthood, Cappadocia would become a center of religious life and thought. Three great saints of the region during the fourth century are outstanding: Saint Gregory (the Theologian) of Nazianzos, from Nenezili in the present-day Aksaray district of Bekârlar (329-394), Saint Gregory of Nyssa (335-394) from the present-day region of Nevşehir, and his brother Saint Basileios [Basil] of Caesarea (329-379), present-day Kayseri. During their time the construction of small churches and monasteries would accelerate, and Christianity would make great strides. Saint Basileios, also known as Saint Basil the Great, was the son of a wealthy family and as such, received a classical education and religious

The location across the Church of Kızılçukur Üzümlü is used as a stum brewery.

instruction, first in Constantinopolis and later in Athens. He decided to go to Caesarea to devote himself to monastic life. Following a period of dallying in monasteries within the boundaries of the empire in Egypt and Syria, he settled in Neo-Caesarea near the Pontus. A pioneer in the establishment of the cenobitic life, communal living in monastic orders, Saint Basil of Caesarea convinced the hermits living sequestered lives to congregate in monasteries, and explained to them that the individual life of seclusion did little to contribute to the common good. The works he wrote on the subject of the cloistered life, theology and ecclesiastical law, along with his exhortations regarding forms of behavior and doctrine, are still valid today in Christian society. For instance, in times of famine Basil urges Christians to break up their single piece of bread and share it, and leave themselves to the protection of the Lord. Basil was not merely a strict man of religion, however, and he gathered the hermits together in monasteries that were not far removed from their settlements, and which provided small cells which they could use as places of spiritual refuge. Elevated to sainthood because of his services to the cause of Christianity, Basil has a special and important place among the fathers of the church. It is for this reason that he is always awarded a deserving position in the center of frescoes. To this day, every year on the 1st and 2nd days of January in Kayseri a special feast day is still celebrated in honor of Saint Basil, who

The refectory of the Monastry of Nuns, Göreme Open Air Museum.

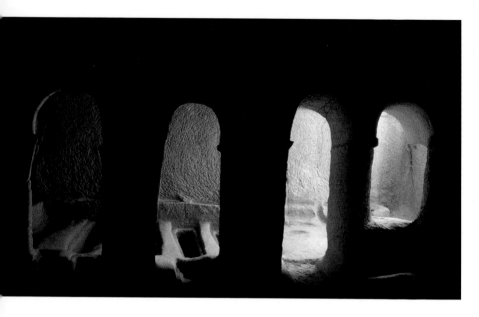

**Tombs of the Church of
Saint Basileios, Göreme.**

died in Cappadocia on the 1st of January 379.

Cappadocia's first monasteries, developed under the leadership of Basil, were small structures built to provide the Christian monks with solitude and a place for meditation. During these difficult years for Christianity, the early monasteries and churches were architecturally quite simple, and were located near sources of water. Daily worship in these small monasteries took place under the supervision of a member of the clergy. The Christians who lived in these structures were unlike the groups in Egypt and Syria who enjoyed a more privileged situation. Everything was shared, the sick were tended, and there were no differences that would cause a rupture with the populace. The greatest reform undertaken by Saint Basil was the practice of common prayer that he instituted in the churches of Göreme. This system would later be maintained in the churches in the Soğanlı, Ihlara, Gömede and Açıksaray valleys. As for Gregory of Nazianzos, like Basil he defended the Greek and Slav position that persons living the cloistered life should not cut themselves off from relations with the world, a concept that influenced the monasteries in the regions of Belisırma, Ihlara and Güzelyurt. This saint, together with Saint Basil, played an important role in the foundation of the Orthodox church.

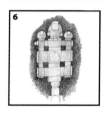

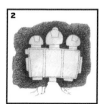

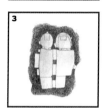

Cappadocian Churches

In general the churches of the Cappadocia Region display five different types of architectural plan:

♦ Lengthways single nave plan: it was used for the barrel vaulted churches with circular apses–some have flat roofs–standardised for Cappadocia. For example: Tokalı I, Karanlık churches in Göreme; Eğritaş, Kokar and Sümbüllü churches in Ihlara; Karşı Church in Gülşehir; Kömürlü Church in Güzelyurt; Nikephoros Phokas Church in Çavuşin–the largest example in the region (chapel plan number 1:29, Göreme)

♦ Widthways rectangular nave plan: churches peculiar to Cappadocia with barrel vaults and two or three apses–a rare example with four apses is Kubbeli II Church in Soğanlı, can be seen in the lower floor. Examples are Saklı, Tokalı II and Yılanlı churches in Göreme (chapel plan number 2:6, Göreme)

♦ Double nave plan: Naves are covered by barrel vaults and and end with an apsis. For example: Pürenli Seki, Kokar (western chapel) churches in Ihlara; Ballı Church in Belisırma; Ioannes Church in Güllüdere. (3: plan of Kırkşehitler Church, Şahinefendi)

♦ Basilical plan: lengthways rectangular plan is divided into three or more naves–middle nave is longer and wider–by parallel colonnades. This plan was used for episcopal churches and the main churches for important monastries. The largest example in the region is Ioannes Prodromos Church in Çavuşin. (4: plan of Durmuş Kadir Church, Avcılar)

♦ Cruciform plan: At the intersection of the arms of the cross stands the central dome. Identified examples mostly have the form of a three-armed-cross; the fourth arm constitutes the apsis. Examples are El Nazar Church in Göreme; Ağaçaltı, Daniel and Yılanlı churches in Ihlara. (5: axonometric perspective Haç Church, Subaşı)

♦ Cross-in-square plan: The floor of this authentic plan of medieval Byzantium is a square. In the middle, the dome carried by four columns extend in four directions as vaults reaching the naos walls and thereby forming the arms of a cross, which constitutes the plan of the upper floor. This plan had its authentic decoration plan as well. Although it was not succesful in the carved churches due to poor lighting, it was tried in some churches because of its strong symbolism. An example is Direkli Church in Belisırma. (6: Kılıçlar Valley Kılıçlar Church number 29, Göreme)

The churches in the Göreme Valley are in general small structures. Most of them can accommodate ten or fifteen people at the most. There are also a few large churches the size of the Tokalı and Karanlık churches that could be used as cathedrals.

The churches in Göreme and environs were constructed by carving them out of the tuff rock that consitutes Cappadocia's natural composition. The widespread single-nave, barrel-vaulted layout was the most appropriate style of architecture for those living in the region and the religious communities, as well as those who had chosen to live in seclusion.

After the carving of the tuff rock had been completed, the walls of these churches—that is to say their rock faces—were plastered with a mixture of straw, tuff and lime. A high proportion of volcanic ash used in the mixture in place of sand gave the walls the appearance of dried clay. The surface of this layer of plaster which was 2-4 mm thick was subsequently colored with different techniques.

Two very different painting techniques can be observed in the Göreme Valley churches. In the first technique, red ochre paint was applied directly to the surface without using plaster or surface coating. In this technique the primary rock surface served as background. In this type of painting seen in churches and chapels of the early Byzantine era, Maltese crosses and geometric and vegetal motifs took a prominent place. However, in later times this type of painting was covered with a plaster mixture and painted with themes appropriate to Christian belief. The Tokalı, St. Basileios, Elmalı and St. Barbara churches in Göreme, the Zelve Valley Balıklı Church and the Ortahisar Fırkatan Church are among the most beautiful examples of this technique.

In the second technique the painting was done on a plaster surface. Two different methods were used. Either the fresco technique was used on wet plaster, or the tempera, or so-called secco technique, was used after the plaster had dried. After the painting was completed, the surface of the fresco was covered with a type of glue derived from plants that gave the paintings a lively quality.

The topics used for the church and chapel frescoes were scenes from the Bible, both the Old and the New Testaments. First and foremost, the life of Jesus and the saints were depicted, but important figures in the religious life of Cappadocia often were to be seen completing other compositions. In general, the immortals were portrayed on the domes, while mortals were depicted on the walls; scenes known as the *Deisis*, which depicted the trio of Jesus, Mary and John the Baptist, occupied the apse.

Apart from the churches adorned with mosaics that were constructed in the name of the emperor in the Byzantine era, the walls and vaults were generally decorated with frescoes, which were less costly to produce and easier in terms of

Right:

Above left, Three Wise Kings, Karanlık Church, Göreme. above right, the Entry into Jerusalem, Karanlık Church, Göreme. below left, Descent of Jesus into Hell, Church of Tatlarin (Kale), Acıgöl. below right, scenes from Tokalı I (Old) Church. Annunciation, Visitation and the Trial by Water.

workmanship. Not all of the wall paintings in the Cappadocia churches were painted by artists. A large number of the incomparably beautiful frescoes were produced by monks.

The topics of the frescoes in the Cappadocia churches were generally arrayed in chronological order: events before and after the birth of Jesus (the Journey to Bethlehem, the Birth of Jesus or Nativity, the Three Wise Kings, the Flight into Egypt...), the miracles performed by Jesus (Healing of the Sick, Raising of Lazarus from the Dead...), and the agony of Christ (the Entry into Jerusalem, the Last Supper, Judas's Betrayal, the Crucifixion, the Ascension...).

Emperor Leon III realized that the influence and power of the monks over the populace was increasing dangerously, and in 726 he forbade the worship of idols; this period of iconoclasm continued until 842. During this era the worship of icons was banned, the frescoes and icons in the churches were destroyed and representation of the human figure was prohibited. Cappadocia was also affected by these prohibitions. Based on the prohibition era, the art of Cappadocia can be divided into three eras as pre-Iconoclastic, Iconoclastic and post-Iconoclastic.

In pre-Iconoclastic Era painting a more linear style prevails. During the Iconoclastic Era, as portrayal of the hu-

Baptism, Karşı Church, Gülşehir.

man figure was forbidden, red ochre paint was used to depict early Christian symbols like crosses, fish and palms. Vaults and ceilings were generally decorated with the cross, a form much revered by the Cappadocians. While the most beautiful examples of Cappadocian painting appeared in the post-Iconoclastic Era, it is a pity that it was impossible to prevent the heavy damage they experienced later. Knowingly or not, many churches were used as dovecotes. With the widening of the windows, wind and rain were able to enlarge the cracks that nature itself had created. As pieces of the frescoes fell, their integrity was compromised. The egg-white that was used in frescoes as a fixative lost its strength over time and the paint layer began to turn to dust; the straw in the stucco disintegrated and it was impossible to prevent blistering and chipping. And to make matters worse, graffiti by shepherds and, particularly, by irresponsible past visitors caused irreparable damage to the frescoes.

In some of the churches one can find hollowed cavities in the form of the familiar tombs that are known to have been used for burial. It was believed that burial inside the church was a guaranteed means to reach heaven. In fact, the carved sarcophagi found in most of these structures were the burial places of the fathers who had helped that particular church and church benefactors.

Right, fresco depicting the benefactor of the church in Karşı Church, Gülşehir.

Opposite page, The Last Supper, Karşı Church, Gülşehir.

STEP-BY-STEP CAPPADOCIA

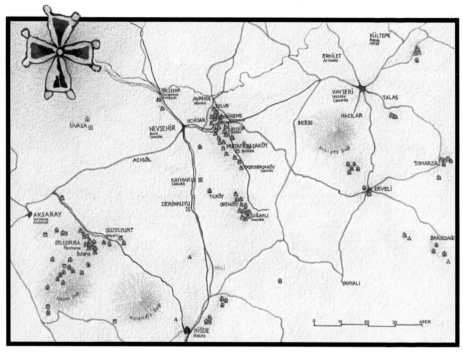

⛰	Rock-cut churches
⌂	Masonry-built churches
🏛	Monastries
⊔	Fortresses
⁝⁝⁝	Underground cities
∴	Hermit cells

**Above, map of rock-cut
churches carved into
tuff rock, masonry-built
churches, fortresses,
underground cities and
hermit cells of Cappadocia.**

**Opposite page, the most
frequently visited sites of
Cappadocia are included
inside a triangle formed
by Avanos, Ürgüp and
Uçhisar.**

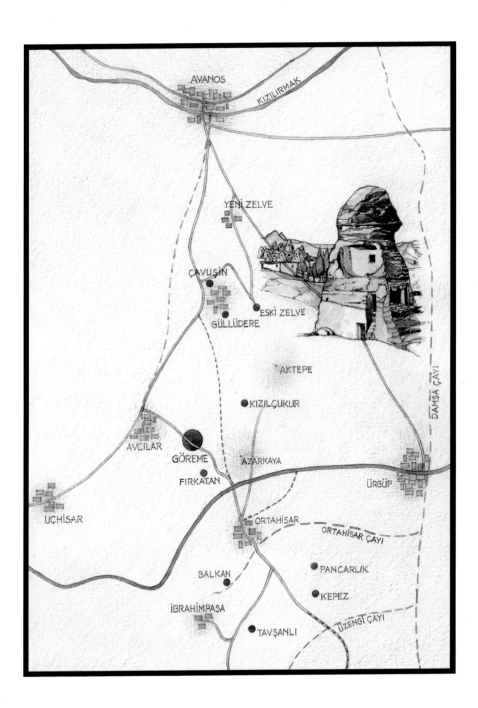

FROM GÖREME TO AVANOS

The incomparable Göreme Valley

Thanks to its unique geological circumstances, the Göreme Valley of Cappadocia is a perfect location for seclusion. Located 17 kilometers from Nevşehir and six kilometers from Ürgüp, its elevation is 1,100 meters above sea level. Although the meaning of the name 'Göreme' is obscure, it is thought that it may originate as a corruption of the name Korama, given by the early Christians who fled from the Arabs and found shelter there. Göreme was the birthplace of the martyred Saint Hieron.

The earliest examples of Byzantine churches can be seen in this valley, which would be used as a location for the education of missionaries. Some researchers propound that Armenians were among the first architects as well. According to these researchers, the tambour and dome at the Halacdere Monastery in Avcılar, at Mavrucan/Güzelöz, is an outstanding example of the domed churches that display the work of Armenian architects. (The tambour is the cylindrical or faceted wall with windows that supports the dome.)

Pages 38-39, view from Göreme Valley.

Opposite page, a look to Göreme Valley.

Below, a fresco layer reveals another layer underneath in Tokalı II (New) Church in Göreme Open Air Museum, Göreme Valley.

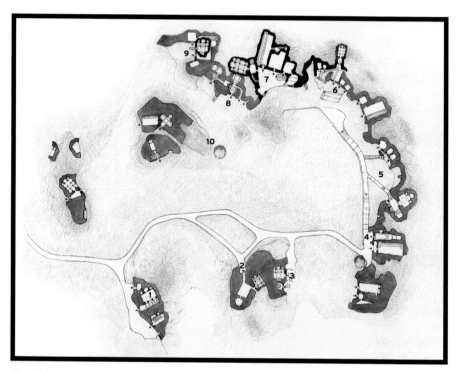

Plan of the Göreme Open Air Museum:

1. Unnamed chapel
2. Elmalı Church
3. Church of Saint Barbara
4. Yılanlı Church
5. and 6. Refectory and hermit cells
7. Karanlık Church
8. Unnamed chapel
9. Çarıklı Church
10. Monastry of Nuns (Kızlar)

Göreme Churches

You can visit numerous churches, many of which contain peerless frescoes, in the present-day Göreme Valley, part of which has been designated an open-air museum. It is believed that there are as many as 200 churches here, including those that are not a part of the museum. The increase in the number of churches occurred when Saint Paul (10-67) decided to make use of this area for the education of missionaries. Some sources maintain that a different church was provided for every day of the year. Unfortunately, a significant number of them were unable to resist the ravages of time and rugged conditions.

In some churches in the region, primarily those in the Ihlara Valley, there are inscriptions that display the date of construction. However, the inscriptions in those of the Göreme Valley have not survived, and it is only possible to date them according to their architectural characteristics or iconography.

We can separate the churches that can be visited into two categories: those within the open-air museum area and those outside it. The churches that are outside the museum limits are the Saklı Kilise [Church], Meryem Ana [the Mother Mary] Church and the Kılıçlar and El Nazar churches.

Below, entrance to the Göreme Open Air Museum.

CHURCHES OF THE GÖREME OPEN AIR MUSEUM

High rock masses, Rahipler ve Rahibeler Manastırı [Monastery of Monks and Nuns] and the St. Basileios Chapel

After purchasing your ticket and beginning your tour, you will see the Monastery of Monks and Nuns on the left. The monastery dates to the eleventh century and consists of a six to seven-storey rock mass. The structure in which all the levels are connected by tunnels consists of a kitchen, dining room, cells and a chapel. For security, heavy sliding rocks were used as a door. There is a chapel on the second floor and a church on the third. The church is domed and contains four columns and three apses.

The most important feature in the nuns' section is the fresco of Jesus executed directly on the rock and the red ornamentation that completes it. The monastery of the monks was unable to resist the forces of time and erosion, and the passages between levels have collapsed.

In the chapel of Saint Basileios near the entrance, the nave and the narthex are separated from one another by two individual galleries. You can also see here graves that have been carved into the chapel.

Right, Saint George is the most popular warrior saint in Byzantine art, Church of Saint Basileios, Göreme.

Opposite page, Monastry of Nuns (Kızlar), Göreme Open Air Museum.

Various eras in the Elmalı Kilise [Apple Church]

Dating from the mid-eleventh to the early twelfth century, the origin of the name of the church (*elma* is apple in Turkish) is not known. The church may have been named for an apple tree in front of its door, or the spot that resembles an apple on one of the columns, or the round object (which is in fact a symbol of the universe) in the hand of the archangel on one of the domes.

One enters the church through a door that is a later addition and a very narrow tunnel. The original door of the church was in a spot directly across from the apse. The Elmalı Kilise has an interesting appearance, with its nine domes, four columns, three apses and the floor plan of an enclosed Greek cross. When one regards the apse from the front, one sees that the primary nave is divided into three sections by the four columns. There are niches on either side of the apse: the *prothesis* on the left, where preparations were made for the mass and where ritual materials were placed, and the *diakonikon* on the right. It is apparent that there was at one time also an iconostasis wall that divided the apse from the nave, but this was destroyed at some time in the past. The Elmalı Kilise,

Below, Elmalı Church, Göreme has a cross-in-square plan.

like many other churches in the valley, has domes, columns and capitals that were carved out of the rock mass. In point of fact, there was no need for columns to support the church. The only reason for the columns was to adhere to the general norms of church architecture and the desire to create an aesthetic appearance.

From beneath certain crumbling frescoes one can discern the primitive and geometric decorations of the Iconoclastic Era. These were later covered with a layer of plaster, and while it was still wet, new frescoes were painted that included representations of the human figure.

The church contains fifteen scenes from the life of Jesus. On the main dome is the Pantocrator Christ (Creator of the Universe and its sole Lord), while angels appear in the other domes. On the walls are scenes portraying the Baptism, the Journey to Jerusalem, the Last Supper, Judas's Betrayal and the Crucifixion. Although some frescoes from the Iconoclastic Era are in good condition, others are in very poor condition.

The columns of Elamlı Church are non-structural, they were built to obey the general form of the architectural form.

Azize Barbara Kilisesi [Church of Saint Barbara], with its symbolic motifs

The Church of Saint Barbara, carved from the continuation of the same rock mass from which the Elmalı Church was carved, dates to the eleventh century. Its shape is cruciform, with two columns, three naves and a single primary apse.

Because the narthex is in ruins, one enters directly into the church, which is one of the most fascinating structures in the Göreme Valley because of its rarely seen symbolic decorations. The examples of symbolic figures and exaggerated motifs are extremely interesting. However, these decorations were not executed during the Iconoclastic Era but were done at a later date inspired by the iconoclastic motifs. There are no churches in Göreme Open Air museum dated to the Iconoclastic Era.

Below and opposite page, brick-red ornamentations in the Church of Saint Barbara enhance the architectural elements such as dome, arches, and vaults.

The painted brick-red figures were applied directly to the rock surface. Some sources maintain that many of the symbols on the walls of this church are involved with sorcery and the breaking of spells to ensure protection against the devil.

At the left side near the entrance we see Saint Barbara

The sites created by carving into rock in the Church of Saint Barbara are accentuated by the lines of ornamentation.

holding a cross in one hand and giving a blessing with the other. Behind her are two martyrs, followed by Saint Gregory and Saint Theodoros and geometric motifs which complete the picture. In the area above the saints there is the figure of a rooster that is pecking at something that resembles a flower, and beneath it, between two crosses, is a strange creature that has risen to its feet. Just as in mythology, the Christians believed that the rooster awoke early in the morning and chased away evil spirits, and that it was a reminder of the desire for a life of freedom. It is believed that the creature that is so difficult to identify beneath the rooster is a symbol of evil, and that in this portrayal it represents the iconoclasts.

It is assumed that the cross designs above the niches known as *prothesis* and *diakonikon* on either side of the apse represent Jesus, and that the four crosses surrounding it represent the four evangelists. The trio of crosses directly above this are believed to represent either the *Deisis* composition of Jesus, Mary and John the Baptist, or the Resurrection composition of Jesus, Moses and Elias. The primary dome is adorned with palm trees, which symbolize long life and immortality. The walls of the church are decorated with different types of crosses: Byzantine, Latin and Maltese.

Yılanlı Kilise [Serpent Church], with its fascinating architecture

This church decorated with frescoes produced in the eleventh century has an interesting architectural form, with neither domes nor columns. The name of the church (*yılan* means serpent in Turkish) is derived from the fresco on the wall to the left of the entrance depicting Saint George and Saint Theodoros killing a serpent in the form of a dragon. On the right of the fresco is Emperor Constantine with his mother Helena and "The True Cross" between them. On the apse wall directly across from the entrance is a depiction of Jesus with a small child being educated in a religious school.

In the fresco on the right-hand wall, we see the most fascinating composition in Yılanlı Kilise. In this fresco Saint Basileios is depicted holding the holy book in his hand. Next to him is Saint Thomas, another of the Cappadocia priests, making a gesture of consecration, with Saint Onuphrius beside him. Onuphrius is said to have remained in the desert for sixty years, subsisting solely on roots and dates, and was later elevated to sainthood. Frescoes of Onuphrius, who was actually of Syrian origin, can also be seen together with Saint Simon, also Syrian, in the Hagia Sophia church in Trabzon, the St. Onuphrius church in Antakya, and the

Far-left, Saints Onuphrius and Thomas, Yılanlı Church, Göreme.

Left, Emperor Constantine and his mother Helena holding the True Cross in between, Yılanlı Church, Göreme.

Church of Saint Gregory of Dikran Honentz in Ani. The feast day of the saint is still celebrated on the twelfth of June. An excavated burial place exists beneath the floorboards of this church as well.

Continuing uphill after leaving the Yılanlı Kilise, a small, cruciform, nameless church whose *iconostasis* is still standing can also be seen. A short distance further on, you will encounter one of the refectories used by the monks. This dining hall contains a table carved from the rock that can accommodate thirty persons, a seat at the head for the abbot, an in-ground cavity for pressing grapes to make wine, and numerous holes and shelves used for various purposes on the walls. The second storey of the structure contains a simple chapel and small rooms.

Below, Saint George and Saint Theodore on horseback battling the dragon, Yılanlı Church, Göreme.

Opposite page, detail from the fresco depicting Saint George and Saint Theodore battling the dragon.

Karanlık Kilise [Dark Church], with magnificent frescoes

This is the most important and magnificent church in the Göreme Valley. Dating to the twelfth to thirteenth centuries, although it was named 'Karanlık' [meaning 'dark' in Turkish] because it was protected naturally for centuries from the ravages of time, light and moisture because of its dark and secluded situation, its frescoes have suffered severe damage because it could not protect itself from the ravages of mankind.

It is necessary to purchase a separate ticket to visit Karanlık Kilise, which only re-opened after a lengthy restoration of its frescoes. But be assured that the superb beauty of its frescoes is well worth the payment of this additional fee.

Karanlık Kilise has a cruciform plan, cross-ribbed vaulting, a central dome, four columns, one central and two small apses, and is entirely carved into the rock. In the entry area, the remains of another church from an earlier era can be seen which, despite being entirely in ruins, has geometric

Opposite page, Karanlık Kilise is the most important and impressive church in the Göreme Valley.

Below, the facade of Karanlık Church.

ornamentation that is still visible. Passing through here, one
enters Karanlık Kilise through a low, narrow door; the frescoes of the church, because of the insufficient light, were executed by making use of mirrors and polished metal placards
to reflect the sunlight.

In the narthex there is a large representation of Mary
and Jesus among the twelve apostles, and the ceiling of the
narthex portrays the Ascension of Jesus, accompanied by four
angels. Directly across from the entrance is a section that was
used during the last years of the church as a burial chamber.

Upon entering the church through the narthex, one
encounters the Nativity scene. In this composition we see
Mary in the center, Jesus in his cradle in the upper right corner,
and in the background, an ox and a donkey. In the cold stable,
the ox and the donkey are warming Jesus with their breath and
by licking him. In the lower right corner we see the first bath
of the baby Jesus, and in the lower left, Saint Joseph regarding
this birth with an expression of amazement. On the interior of
the vault directly above this scene we see the Three Wise Kings
presenting their gifts of gold, frankincense (an incense made
from the resin of the *Boswellia* tree) and myrrh. Next to this
composition are the four Evangelists, Matthew, Mark, Luke
and John, portrayed writing their sacred books. The Lord of
the Universe, or Pantocrator Christ, is displayed in almost all
the churches in the most central location at the highest point.
Jesus is portrayed making a gesture of blessing with one hand

Opposite page, Transfiguration, Karanlık Church.

Above left, Nativity, Karanlık Church.

Above right, Judas's Betrayal, Karanlık Church.

Left, the portrayal of Pantocrator Christ in the eastern dome of Karanlık Church.

while holding the Holy Bible in the other. The message of the Pantocrator Christ is that Jesus is both the Creator and the Savior. Another important scene is that of the *Deisis*, the Pantocrator Christ with Mary and John the Baptist on either side. The *Deisis* frescoes portray Mary and John the Baptist in supplication to Jesus for the forgiveness of the sins of mankind on the Day of Judgment. The *Deisis* fresco in Karanlık Kilise is located in the upper part of the apse, within a semicircular niche.

Above the niche wall on the right side that is known as the *diakonikon* is the scene of Jesus and his apostles at the Last Supper. The fish in the center of the table is the symbol of Jesus and Christianity, which is derived from the ancient Greek word for fish, IKTUS. The letters consist of the first letters of five different words: I/İesus-Jesus, K/Kristus, T/Teus, U/

Uilius, S/Soter, which together represent, 'Jesus Christ, Son of God, Savior.'

To the right is the scene of the *Anastasis*, or Resurrection, portraying Jesus raising Adam and Eve to Heaven, with the devil, symbolizing the watchman to Hell, cowering beneath the feet of Jesus with his hands tied. Next to the broken gates of Hell we can see its locks and nails scattered on the ground. The same wall contains a fresco of the Crucifixion of Jesus on the Hill of Golgotha. The right side of the chest of Jesus has been pierced by the spear of the Roman soldier in front of Him, and is bleeding. On the other side the Virgin Mary, his sister Myriam (wife of Cleophas) and Mary Magdalene are weeping. A second soldier to the left of Jesus is holding out to Him on the end of his spear a sponge soaked in vinegar to further increase His thirst. On either side of the cross are red and grey-colored balls symbolizing the sun and the moon. Directly above this fresco is the scene of the Betrayal of Jesus, and along the same wall are scenes depicting three angels and the miracle of the Raising of Lazarus from the Dead. Immediately above the door is the scene of Jesus, garbed in white, returning to the world in Resurrection, and in the vault directly beneath it are scenes showing the Entry of Jesus to Jerusalem. In this fresco Jesus is astride a donkey and people have removed their outer garments and spread them on the ground in the donkey's path. In the fresco of the Baptism, the entire body of Jesus is immersed in the River Jordan. While John is baptizing Him, a dove alights on the head of Jesus. The dove symbolizes the Holy Spirit, a member of the Holy Trinity sacred to Christianity. In another composition we see Mary and the Child Jesus in the scene of the Flight into Egypt.

Uppermost and opposite page, Crucifixion, Karanlık Church.

Above, Last Supper, Karanlık Church.

Çarıklı Kilise [Church of the Sandal], a structure on the heights

This is the smallest of the churches with columns in the Göreme Valley, with a cruciform shape, two columns, four arches, three apses and a barrel vault. The church is in a high location, and is reached by stairs. The lower storeys contain cells, a dining hall and a meeting room. From the aspect of its design it resembles the Church of Saint Barbara. Because the church was visited so frequently in the past, it is thought that a piece of the True Cross may have been preserved here. The church was named 'Çarıklı' by the locals because the sandals of the saints resembled the shoes known as *çarık* that is worn in the region. In addition to this explanation, under the present-day floor covering are two footprints that may also be shown as a reason for this name. The church's thirteenth-century frescoes show a similarity to those in the Karanlık and Elmalı churches.

Opposite page and below, the smallest of the churches with columns in the Göreme Valley is Çarıklı Church, which has the cross-in-square plan.

If you stand facing the apsis, you can see at the right of two small domes on the ceiling a depiction of Simon of Kirene carrying on his back the cross on which Christ would be crucified on Golgotha; this is the only representation of this scene to be found in all the churches of Göreme. The Pantocrator Christ in the central dome is surrounded by five angels within medallions, and the four Evangelists are portrayed in the pendentives.

On the west wall of the church we see the important benefactors of the church: Theognostos, Leon, Michel and Simon. Çarıklı Church contains other frescoes as well: the Crucifixion, Descent from the Cross, the Raising of Lazarus from the Dead, Childhood of Jesus, Entry into Jerusalem and the Resurrection.

In the dining room located on the storey beneath the church, on the wall at the end that was reserved for the abbot, is the scene of the Last Supper.

Tokalı Kilise [Buckle Church], largest in the region

The largest church in the region, Tokalı Kilise is reminiscent of a cathedral. It is composed of three segments that were constructed at different periods: the old, single-nave church, the new church and the oldest church that was used as a cemetery. In addition, the chapel inside the new church could be considered a separate section on its own.

The old barrel-vaulted and single-nave church appears to extend like a corridor along the building's primary axis, but a careful examination reveals that the original plan was cruciform. When the new section was added to the eastern side, the apse of the old church was destroyed.

On the ceiling of the old church, which dates to the tenth century, from right to left there is a procession of scenes from the life of Jesus, from the Nativity to the Ascension. All of these scenes are taken from the New Testament.

On the right side are the scenes of Annunciation, the Visitation, the Trial by Water, the Journey to Bethlehem and the Nativity; on the left side the Three Wise Kings, the Massacre of the Innocents, the Flight to Egypt, and the Assassination of Zechariah.

Scenes from the life of Jesus are arranged successively in the ceiling of Tokalı I (Old) Church.

On the right side of the center zone are scenes of the Pursuit of Elizabeth, the Encounter of Jesus with John the Baptist, the Baptism of Jesus and the Wedding at Cana.

To the left of center are the Miracle of the Wine, Petrus and Andreas meeting Jesus and believing in Him in the Tiberiard Desert, Loaves and Fishes, the Appointment of the Apostles, the Healing of the Blind Man, Raising of Lazarus from the Dead; on the right, on lower panel are the Entry to Jerusalem, the Last Supper, Judas's Betrayal, Jesus before Pilatus; on the left, on lower panel are Simon of Kirene on the Road to Calvary, the Crucified Jesus, the Descent from the Cross, the Burial of Jesus, the Women at the Empty Grave, the Descent of Jesus to Hell and over the entrance is the Transfiguration. In addition there are frescoes of Saint Gregorios, the apostles and other saints.

The new church has a rectangular plan, a single narthex and a single corridor, and dates to the late tenth to early eleventh century. The most important characteristic of the new church is the range of the prevailing colors of its frescoes: blue of lapis lazuli, green, red and brown. The quality and beauty of the colors is almost never seen in other Cappadocian

Above, scenes from the life of Jesus in Tokalı I (Old) Church.

Uppermost left, Descent from the Cross. Uppermost right, Flight of the Holy Family to Egypt, Tokalı I(Old) Church. Above left, Entry into Jerusalem, Tokalı I(Old) Church. Above right, Adoration of the Three Wise Kings, Tokalı I(Old) Church.

churches. The apse is separated from the nave by the columns which serve as the iconostas.

The parekklesion on the left, the chapel that is adjacent to the church but forms a separate section, has been carved out of the rock. There is no second section on the right.

The topics of the frescoes in the new church are rich and fascinating. The Annunciation, the Visitation, Joseph's questioning of Mary, the Journey to Bethlehem, the Dream of Joseph, the Nativity, the Wise Kings, the Flight to Egypt, the Presentation of Jesus to the Scholars at the Temple, the calling of John the Baptist, miracles like the Wedding at Cana, where Jesus turned water into wine, the Feast of Passover, when Jesus multiplied loaves and fishes, the Apostles' walk on the water of the Sea of Galilee, the Healing of the Lepers, the Healing of the rich man's son, the Healing of the paralytic, the Raising of Lazarus from the Dead, along with scenes from the Passion such as Christ's Entry to Jerusalem, Jesus on the road to Golgotha, the Crucifixion, Mary among the angels, the Descent from the Cross, the Women in front of the Empty Grave, Christ's Descent into Hell with John the Baptist in the company of the prophets David and Solomon and Mary's Assumption into Heaven are among the wealth of topics that have been portrayed in the frescoes.

In the lower part of the apse one can also see among the important men of religion Saint John Chrysostom, Saint Gregory of Nazianzos and Saint Nicholas of Myra.

Below, Tokalı II (New) Church has a lengthways rectangular plan.

Opposite page, on the column arches of Tokalı II (New) Church, over the blue of lapislazuli ground, on the left is the Emperor Constantine holding a staff and a globe and his wife Helena across him in Tokalı II (New) Church. On the corridor ceiling are the priests holding the Bible in roundrels; on the apsis arch, in the middle stands an unidentified angel with Ezekilel and Yeremya on either side.

GÖREME CHURCHES OUTSIDE THE OPEN AIR MUSEUM

Saklı Kilise [Hidden Church], hidden for many years

The eleventh century Saklı Kilise was discovered by coincidence many years after landslides had covered its entrance. The church originally had three apses, but today only one apse remains. Because the structure had been hidden under the earth for so many years it has been called the Hidden Church. It is located approximately 300 meters from the Göreme Valley in the direction of Avcılar. Because it is on the side of a hill it is not easy to see from a distance; you will have to look a bit for it.

The topics of the frescoes are of a discernible quality. Among them are scenes of the Annunciation, Nativity, Presentation at the Temple and Crucifixion. On the west wall we see the Ascension and Transfiguration, while on the south wall, among the important saints are John Chrysostom (John of the 'golden mouth'), Nicholas, bishop of Myra (whose face has been damaged) with St. Blaise (Vlas) of Sebastea (present-day Sivas), the Emperor Constantine and his mother Helena. On the arch of the south apse is the scene of the *Deisis* (Supplication). Saints John the Baptist, Epiphanius and Gregorios are depicted in the north apse.

Frescoes depicting scenes from the life of Jesus in Saklı Church.

Meryem Ana Kilisesi [Church of Mary Mother of God], with its beautiful view

When coming from Avcılar towards the Göreme Valley, on the hill to the left of Tokalı Kilise, approximately 250 meters away, is Meryem Ana Kilisesi, which is somewhat difficult to see. The view of the Kılıçlar Valley from this church is quite beautiful. Its entry door, which has suffered serious damage from erosion, is approximately thirty meters lower. Right next to the entrance is a heavy stone in the shape of a wheel that was used as a door. It is believed that the tunnel here was excavated in order to connect it with another church. The stone is also thought to have provided security by blocking the entrance as we know the region was at times extremely vulnerable to external attacts. The dovecotes formed by covering of the entrance and window bays of the church are also noteworthy.

Depictions of Mary in the Church of Mary, Kılıçlar Valley, Göreme.

Kılıçlar Kilise [Church of Swords], with the Ascension dome

The columns in Kılıçlar Church are carved into the main tuff rock like carving of a statue from stone, Kılıçlar Valley, Göreme.

The church is located approximately 600 meters north of the Göreme Valley. It has a cruciform floor plan, three apses and four columns. The central dome contains a fresco of the Ascension, and on the other domes Jesus has been depicted, while on the ceilings we see the archangels Gabriel and Michael. The church dates to the ninth to tenth centuries.

El Nazar Kilisesi [Church of St. Anargiros], in the midst of nature

This is a church hidden among the vineyards between Avcılar and Göreme. In some places one can follow the traces of the old riverbed that lead to the church. The church dates to the late tenth to early eleventh centuries, and consists of two storeys, the upper storey of which is in ruins. The structure has a 'T' shape, with a central dome and three apses.

In addition to the frescoes inside the church, the appearance of the church in its natural setting is quite beautiful as well. On the walls are large representations of major events such as the childhood of Jesus, the Resurrection, the Nativity and the Crucifixion. In addition, there are frescoes of the saints, the Annunciation, the Visitation, the Presentation at the Temple, the Baptism, the Raising of Lazarus from the Dead, Entry into Jerusalem and Ascension, as well as portraits of unnamed saints in medallions. The draftsmanship and colors of the frescoes are exceptional and quite beautiful.

El Nazar Church has cruciform plan, Göreme.

The Fairy Chimneys of Avcılar

Avcılar, or Matiana as it was formerly called, is approximately 1 kilometer from the Göreme churches. Avcılar Village was first called Korama, then Göreme, but elders have not forgotten the name Avcılar. Unfortunately the churches in this village with such beautiful fairy chimneys are not in good condition. The conical rock structures that were carved for use as burial places during the Roman Era are now used for such domestic purposes as houses and storage depots.

Çavuşin landscapes

The pleasure of walking at Çavuşin

Life in the carved houses of the village of Çavuşin, five kilometers from the Göreme Valley, continued until 1960. This village and its close environs offer a wide range of alternatives for walkers and hikers in its exceptional natural landscapes. You can take a two-hour walk starting from the Ürgüp-Nevşehir highway in the Kızılçukur Valley. Güllüdere, which you can reach by passing through the village of Çavuşin, is another natural wonder that was used hundreds of years ago by monks as a place of retreat. A walk in the Akvadi, also close to Çavuşin, is another interesting alternative.

You can have a two-hour-walking tour in Kızılçukur Valley.

Çavuşin churches

Of the twelve churches in the vicinity of Çavuşin, the most important one is Büyük Güvercinlik Kilisesi [Grand Dovecote Church], built in 964-965 by the Byzantine Emperor Nicophoras Phokas for the soldiers and heroes who played an important role in achieving his victory over the Arab armies. The structure has a single nave and barrel vaulting; its narthex is now in ruins. Scenes from the childhood of Jesus can be seen on the arches of the church. On the east wall there are frescoes of the Blessing of the Apostles and the Ascension, along with angels and saints. There is an interesting fresco on the north wall depicting The Dreams of St. Eustathios. The church also contains depictions of prophets, saints and angels and some of the forty Christians who were martyred by the Romans in Sebasteia (Sivas). Jesus is depicted on the dome of the church, where there are balls of fire burning on His left side while those on His right have been extinguished. Immediately below this is a series of blue and green portraits of saints whose faces have been erased. Constantine is also portrayed wearing his imperial garments alongside his mother Helen and Saint

Below, numerous connected locations carved into the big tuff hills in Çavuşin...

Opposite page, Great Church of Güvercinlik.

Blaise. Revered as a healer and also the patron saint of domestic animals, during the fourth-century massacres in the vicinity of Mount Erciyes during the reign of Licinius, Saint Blaise healed countless people, and is among the most beloved saints of this region. On the north side of the apse you can see the benefactor of the church, Nicophoras Phokas, with his empress Theophano beside him. The list of the church's rich collection of frescoes is complete with the compositions of the Childhood of Mary (between two angels), the Transfiguration, Jesus between Moses and Elias, Saint Peter, Saint John and Saint James.

There is another church in Çavuşin that is believed to be dedicated to John the Baptist. While the church is dated to the late fifth to early sixth century, the frescoes were painted in the ninth century. The scenes relate important events in the life of Jesus, such as the Baptism, Transfiguration, Crucifixion, Annunciation, Visitation, Nativity and the Betrayal by Judas.

If you continue in the direction of Avanos you can see another church, which is called the Dovecote. This church without columns is in rather poor condition due to erosion, and its frescoes are in tones of green and brown.

Opposite page, the fresco in Grand Dovecote Church which depicts the scenes from the life of Jesus successively.

Below, the Church of John the Baptist dates to 5-6th. centuries.

Zelve (Paşabağ), center of the Fairy Chimneys,

Life in the Zelve Valley, which was one of the important set-tlements in the region from the fourth until the thirteenth centuries, continued until 1952. It is generally acknowledged that the variety of large, small, conical, pyramid-shaped, pointed or blunt fairy chimneys in Zelve are the most beauti-ful in the region. Zelve presents a picture of abandonment of a village that still existed until a short time ago, with a Seljuk-type mosque and adjacent homes carved from the rock, some of which still resist the ravages of time.

Although their frescoes are in a very decrepit state, the churches of Balıklı, Üzümlü and Geyikli are the im-portant ecclesiastical structures that are still standing in this valley. Balıklı Kilise is dedicated to the Syrian Saint Simeon Stylites who spent a large part of his life as a hermit atop a column. It is said that during the fifth century, the Hermit Simeon spent his life of seclusion in the Paşabağ's forest of fairy chimneys, in a tiny cell at the very top of one of these natural wonders with three crowns. On the walls of Balıklı Kilise one can also see saints, young Daniel among the lions and the youth thrown into the furnace, and on the ceiling, Constantine (holding a cross in his hands) and Helena and the prophets David and Solomon.

Below, type of fairy chimneys with three caps stemming from a single body, Zelve (Paşabağ).

Opposite page, a fairy chimney with three caps stemming from a single body, Zelve (Paşabağ).

Avanos, brought to life by the Kızılırmak River

Avanos rests against the mountain İğdiş Dağı, divided in two by the Kızılırmak River which passes through it. This district in the center of mystical Cappadocia has an atmosphere that is all its own. Avanos was an important transit point during the Hittite Era, became one of the settlements of repute in the region during the Roman Era, and later again became an important transit point during the Byzantine and Seljuk eras. The oldest known name of the city is Venessa, which means 'city'. The Evranosoğulları Beyliği, who settled there during the Seljuk Era, later gave their name to the settlement, which was corrupted to Avanos over the course of time. As the historian Strabon related in his renowned *Geographica*, which he wrote between the latter 1st. century BC. and the beginning of the 1st. century AD., Avanos or Venessa was the third largest settlement in the area after Kayseri (Caesarea) and Kemerhisar.

The famous stone bridge of Avanos. It was started to be built in 1898 by the contribution of Kurena Arif Bey of Avanos, who was an official at the court of Sultan Abdülhamit, and was inaugurated in 1900. The bridge, which cost 3700 lira back then, rests on total of 11 supports, together with the bridgeheads on either side. The supports of the bridge were changed in 1924, resulting in concrete ones. The concrete parts were built under the supervision of an Hungarian named Wolf, with the help of Turkish craftsmen.

Located 18 kilometers from Ürgüp, Avanos is the third leg of the triangle of Avanos, Ürgüp and Göreme, the most important tourist destinations in the region. With its pottery, eleagnus [*iğde*] and apricot trees, its old houses, history and geography, the most distinguising feature of this pleasant Anatolian town is the Kızılırmak River that has flowed unceasingly for millions of years. The Kızılırmak has the greatest capacity of any of Turkey's rivers; while it struggles to cope with pollution on the one hand, on the other it continues to bestow its bounty on the fields of beets, potatoes, onions and fruit orchards.

Architectural treasures of Avanos

Like every other corner of Cappadocia, Avanos provided refuge to thousands of Christians trying to escape from religious persecution by the Romans. Yamanlı Kilise is one of the oldest in the region, and visiting religious groups can still worship there. Worship also continues at the thirteenth-century Seljuk Alaeddin Mosque in Avanos. There is a wealth of history hidden in the substructure of this county seat, beginning in the Orta Mahalle [Neighborhood] and extending to the Alaeddin Mahallesi: one of the region's numerous underground cities is located here. There are still old houses from the Ottoman Era towering over the underground city. If you continue past these houses towards the town center, you will see next to the bridge a mansion dating to 1902, the Doktor Hacı Nuri Bey Konağı, a magnificent structure unique to the region that has been the subject of research and books.

The historical stone bridge connecting the two banks of the Kızılırmak was constructed in the year 1900. The bridge rests on eleven supports, and was constructed with the contribution of Kurena Arif Bey, an official at the court of Sultan Abdülhamid. The second bridge over the Kızılırmak, one of Turkey's first suspension bridges, is only open to pedestrian traffic.

One of the most beautiful examples of civil architecture in Avanos, Dr. Hacı Nuri Bey Mansion, built in 1902.

Avanos pottery

Ceramics, pottery and carpet weaving have been the most important sources of revenue for this settlement for centuries. Avanos is the location of one of Anatolia's most distinctive pottery workshops. The present-day residents of Avanos, like their predecessors since Hittite times, continue to make pottery with the red clay removed from the bed of the Kızılırmak River, using simple foot-powered wheels and their handicraft to create clay forms that are one more beautiful than the other. The shores of the Kızılırmak are full of pottery workshops, and almost all of the potters are continuing the work of their fathers.

You can watch the pottery demonstrations in pottery ateliers of Avanos.

Saruhan Caravanserai, an unusual Seljuk building

Located approximately five kilometers from Avanos along the new Kayseri road, the Saruhan Caravanserai was commissioned in 1249 by the Seljuk Sultan İzzeddin Keykavus II. It is one of the largest caravanserais in Central Anatolia, covering a space of 2,000 square meters. Ornamented with the geometric designs that are typical of Seljuk architecture and art, its front portal is one of the most magnificent features of this caravanserai that resembles a castle. Unlike other Seljuk caravanserais in which the *mescit*, or small mosque, is located in the center of the courtyard, here it was constructed above the portal. The area to the right of the courtyard contains a Turkish bath and rooms reserved for special guests. Above the large covered section in which the animals were quartered on one side and the caravan members on the other, rises a dome in the form of a cupola.

Çeç Tumulus preserves its secrets

The Çeç Tumulus, one of the largest tumuluses in Anatolia, is the most famous one among the various tumuleses between Avanos and Özkonak, and it is the one we are least informed about. This artificial hill 32 meters in height is made of broken stone and resembles a small mountain; it is probable that it contains the grave of one of the Cappadocian kings, but it has not been excavated or researched up until this time. Some researchers maintain that the Çeç Tumulus, which does not belong to Phrygian or Lydian civilizations that were famous for their tumuleses and is not known by whom it was built, could be a sacred place. It is a smaller version of the Nemrut Tumulus in the vicinity of Adıyaman, and traces of a road with stairs can still be seen extending to its peak. The Çeç Tumulus, which has a majestic form that can compete with other great king tombs, can be approached by car up to a certain point, after which it is necessary to continue on foot.

CAPPADOCIA "CITADELS"

Uçhisar, a hilltop view of Cappadocia

Uçhisar is Cappadocia's highest hill, and is located twelve kilometers from Ürgüp and ten kilometers from Nevşehir.

The natural aspect of Uçhisar Kalesi [Fortress] presents a beautiful sight. Its solid and powerful situation provided a significant advantage in defense against the Arab invasions. The view from Uçhisar Fortress offers a magnificent panorama of the region and of Mount Erciyes, located 80 kilometers away. There is an old cave inside the fortress, and the houses of Uçhisar rest against the outskirts of the it.

Uçhisar is one of the best locations from which to view the dovecotes, one of Cappadocia's most distinctive features.

Below, the highest hill of Cappadocia, Uçhisar.

Opposite page, some of the Uçhisar fairy chimneys, used once as dovecotes by the farmers of Uçhisar, are at present used as guest houses.

Ortahisar, a rock-fortress on the heights

Along the Ürgüp-Nevşehir highway, about six kilometers before Ürgüp there is a turnoff for Ortahisar. The fortress on the mass of natural rock, used by the early Christians who settled here as a shelter and a refuge, is the most majestic location in the settlement and the second highest point in the region.

Behind the Ortahisar Fortress in the deserted old neighborhoods are the provisions depots that have been in use since Byzantine times. Every year tons of lemons, oranges and citrus fruits are brought here from the Mediterranean region, chiefly Mersin, for storage in the natural depots in Ortahisar before being exported to Europe.

In the vicinity of Ortahisar are the Üzümlü, Sarıca and Cambazlı churches. The valley below the settlement extends as far as İbrahimpaşa Village, and boasts one of the most beautiful walking courses in all of Cappadocia.

The fortress in Ortahisar which is on the natural rock mass, is the second highest point of the region.

Pancarlık Kilisesi [Church of Saint Theodoros], a unique structure

Located in the south of the district along the vineyard road to Mustafapaşa, Pancarlık Kilisesi, dedicated to Saint Theodoros, is one of Cappadocia's oldest and most unique churches. Dating to the eleventh century, Pancarlık Kilisesi is situated inside a huge rock mass; it has a single nave, a single apse and flat ceiling. The color green predominates in its frescoes, which relate biblical scenes.

Left above, Journey to Bethlehem, Pancarlık Church.

Left below, view of Pancarlık Church from a distance.

UNDERGROUND CITIES

Underground refuges

Of the currently-known 36 underground cities of Cappadocia, the ones that are open to visitors are Derinkuyu, Kaymaklı, Özkonak, Mucur, Örentepe, Gümüşkent, Gelveri, Tatlarin and Acıgöl. These settlements were of enormous value to the development of Christianity as they provided the early Christians with a place to hide, shelter and worship, and were in use until the end of the seventh century. Because they were deserted in the centuries that followed, with the passage of time they were filled with deposits of soil from rain and flooding. There are other underground cities in the region today that have not yet been uncovered.

It is not known precisely how long these underground cities resembling giant ants' nests were occupied or by how many people, and any idea on the subject cannot proceed further than guesswork. However, it is acknowledged that large cities like Derinkuyu and Kaymaklı accommodated a population of approximately 4,000.

When the upper and lower floors of Derinkuyu underground city are compared, the upper floors are rough and disorganized in plan, whereas lower floors are planned and supported by columns. This obviously indicates that here

A view from Derinkuyu underground city.

lived different people of different ages.

To construct the underground cities it was necessary to choose points where the volcanic tuff layer was soft and easy to excavate. The south, east and west sides of high hills were chosen for these settlements; because winter months in the region are very cold and snowy, the north faces of the hills were not used. The temperatures of both summer and winter months in the underground cities were reasonable. One of the most important issues in the underground cities was ventilation. To solve this problem, first ventilation shafts 70-80 meters deep were dug, then the galleries and rooms that would constitute the city were excavated. The removal of soil and debris in the course of excavation was another important issue. It is believed that the piles of debris and soil dumped into the valleys was lost with erosion. One descended to lower storeys in the underground cities by small inclinations, which gradually deepened, and at the base of the ventilation chimneys would be wells for water.

Small towns were founded above some of the underground cities. It is conjectured that these people who lived under constant threat became accustomed to living in the face of enemy hordes, and that they were able to warn one another of oncoming danger by means of a system of smoke signals

The church with two naves and apses is in Kaymaklı underground city.

The kitchen on the third storey in Kaymaklı underground city.

and mirrors that they had established on the heights. Large heavy cylindrical rocks were used as doors at the entrances of tunnels to guard against danger; once in place, these doors could only be opened from the inside.

Because the corridors that connected the various floors are only 1.6 to 1.7 meters in height, it is supposed that this was because either the inhabitants were rather short in height or because of the desire to make the excavation easier. In addition, there were holes for communication between levels that were 3-4 meters long and about 10 centimeters in diameter.

Only a few kitchens have been discovered in the underground cities. The people who stayed in these cities were living in the manner of small family groups, and collective kitchens were envisioned. It is also likely that, in order to prevent smoke from cooking fires being detected, cold foods were generally consumed. However, traces of smoke can be clearly seen on the walls of the rooms used as kitchens in the underground cities.

The first storeys of the underground cities were usually devoted to the animals. And like the depots for the storage of foodstuffs, caves for storing wine were not forgotten.

Derinkuyu, Cappadocia's largest underground city

The district of Derinkuyu is at an elevation of 1,350 meters above sea level, and is located 29 km from Nevşehir, 50 km from Niğde and 80 km from Aksaray, in the bowl-shaped volcanic Misli Ovası [Plain] between Mount Erciyes and the Hasan Dağları [Mountains]. The effects of erosion on the sandy soil of the district are very powerful. Derinkuyu and its environs bear rich traces of the Hittite, Phrygian, Roman and Byzantine eras. Underground cities, a mental institution, churches, missionary schools and a baptismal font have been uncovered within the limits of the district.

Named Derinkuyu [deep well] because in the past the drinking water was obtained from wells 60-70 meters deep and because of its antique underground city, the district is home to Cappadocia's largest eight-storey underground city. The settlement came to light completely by coincidence in 1967, and was opened to visitors after cleanup work had been completed.

It is believed that the first floor, which dates to the Hittite Era, was used as a storage area, and that the other

The stable on the first storey of Derinkuyu underground city.

floors were excavated together when the need increased in later times. The second floor houses a kitchen, refectory, cellars, school, baptismal font and depots. The third and fourth floors were used as places of hiding. In the face of danger, the lower floors were more secure. Although it is estimated that the tunnel that begins on the third floor of Derinkuyu extends 9 kilometers to the underground city of Kaymaklı, there is no evidence about existence of such a tunnel. On the lower floors we find a meeting room with three columns, graves, shafts for ventilation and emergency warnings, and water wells. The ventilation is ensured by 52 shafts 70-80 meters deep. On the eighth floor there is a cruciform church that is 10 meters wide, 8.5 meters long, 2.5 meters high.

Derinkuyu's stone doors are 55-65 cm thick, 1.70-1.75 m in diameter and weight 300 to 500 kilos. It is believed that these doors were carved in their original place when the city was being built.

Opposite page, the long tunnel in Derinkuyu underground city, which permits passage to the locations on lower storeys.

Left, the location with a sliding stone used to control the passage through, Derinkuyu underground city.

Kaymaklı underground city, beneath a cemetery

Kaymaklı is 20 km from Nevşehir, and 9 km from Derinkuyu. The city's old name of Enegüp was changed by the Anatolian Greeks to Enegobi, and changed again after 1924 by the Turks to Kaymaklı.

The typology of the entry floor of underground city can be dated to the Early Byzantine Era. Kaymakli was discovered in 1964 and is estimated to be 20 meters deep; it is possible to tour the first four storeys. The four storeys of the city that have been cleaned and opened to visitors contain depots for food and wine, a church, ventilation shafts, water wells and round cylindrical doors. The doors, 55–60 cm thick, 1.70–1.75 m high and weighing 500 kilos, can only be opened from the inside. The rooms are connected to one another by narrow corridors.

There was a cemetery above the city. Because not all the storeys of Kaymaklı have been cleaned out, it is not possible to visit the entire city. There is only a single kitchen on the first floors. On the second floor of this underground city are hollows that were used as graves.

The stable at the entrance of Kaymaklı underground city.

Mazı Köyü, sheepfolds in the underground city of Mazata

The underground city of Mazata, located 18 km from Ürgüp and 10 km from Kaymaklı, is one of the locales that has not yet been entirely cleaned and opened to visitors. To date, four entrances have been discovered, but the size of the underground city and the number of its storeys is still unclear. The presence of a number of sheepfolds on the first floor is an indication of the importance of animal husbandry here. In addition to depots for provisions and caves for storing wine, the Mazata underground city also has a lovely church. The Roman Era graves carved into the rock on the hills of Mazı Köyü are quite interesting. The church and most of the chapels in the valley of the Bağırsak Stream were unfortunately flooded, and there is only one that is in good condition. This church with a single column has decorations of crosses on its walls.

Tatlarin underground city, with its well-developed substructure

Tatlarin Köyü, with a population of 3,500, is located 20 km from Nevşehir and 9 km from Acıgöl, and is one of the settlements that harbors an underground city. The underground city rests within a large mass of rock known as the *kale*, or fortress, and was opened to visitors in 1991. Unlike other underground cities in Cappadocia, it has both toilets and cesspools. In addition, the ventilation shafts, kitchen and depots are clearly visible in the huge rock mass that is home to the underground city, and there are many Byzantine Era churches in its vicinity. It is a pity that the majority of these churches are in ruins. Most of the frescoes that adorned their walls have been darkened and erased by soot from the hearths that burned in their time.

Özkonak underground city and its doors

Özkonak, located 14 km from Avanos, can be reached via a turnoff on the Avanos-Gülşehir road. The underground city was discovered in 1972 by a landowner, Latif Acer, while working in the garden of his home. Cleaned and opened to visitors in 1973, it was formally declared an open air museum by the Ministry of Culture in 1990. The Özkonak underground city, which contains a dining hall, chapel, ventilation tunnel, well and depots for storing supples and wine, has interesting cylindrical wheel-shaped doors that are 60 cm thick, 1.7 meter in diameter and weigh 500 kilos. Unlike the doors in other underground cities, it is clear that they were produced inside this underground city.

The Özkonak vicinity is also home to the Yalı Damı Shelter and the Byzantine-era Belha Monastery. In addition, it hosts three large tumuluses of the Roman Era.

Acıgöl, Cappadocia's smallest underground city

The underground city in the town of Acıgöl, located along the Nevşehir-Aksaray road, is the smallest and easiest to tour of the underground cities that are open to visitors in the Cappadocia region. Traces of the antique Hittite city of Topada can still be seen in the vicinity of Acıgöl. Among the most important and interesting sights is the Hittite inscription carved into a large rock mass within the boundaries of the village of Ağıllı Köyü.

This inscription dates to the era of the Hittite Tabal Principality that governed Cappadocia between 1200 and 700 BC; it relates in Hittite hieroglyphics the sacrifices made by the king to the gods and his gratitude to them.

Opposite page, Hittite hierogliph inscription, Topada, Acıgöl.

FROM ÜRGÜP TO SOĞANLI

Ürgüp, one of Cappadocia's oldest settlements

Pages 102-103, engraving by the French traveller Charles Texier, 1844.

Below, general view of Ürgüp.

Opposite page, examples of civil architecture in Ürgüp.

Ürgüp lies 20 kilometers east of Nevşehir, and is another of Cappadocia's oldest and most important settlements. Up until 1924 a large part of its population consisted of Orthodox Greeks. Named Osiana during the Byzantine era, in later years it was named after the Christian Saint Prokopios, who was born and died here. After falling under Seljuk dominion in the eleventh century, it took the name Başhisar, and it is home to two tombs dating to the Seljuk Era. The one named Altı Kapılı, [With Six Doors] is the tomb of a noblewoman and her daughter. The tomb named Kılıçaslan is located on the hilltop of Temenni Tepesi. During the nineteenth century Ürgüp, renowned today as one one of Cappadocia's most important centers of tourism, was famed in Central Anatolia for its libraries, mosques, churches, fountains and intellectual life.

Sinassos (Mustafapaşa), fine examples of Anatolian Greek architecture

Six kilometers from Ürgüp, Mustafapaşa is a pleasant old *Rum* [Anatolian Greek] village that possesses the finest examples of Rum civilian architecture in the region. The Orthodox Greeks who lived here until the population exchanges of 1924 were owners of beautiful late nineteenth- and early twentieth-century homes, churches and wineries, making it one of Cappadocia's wealthiest and most prosperous villages. During the winter months the men of Sinassos, as it was then known, occupied themselves in Istanbul with the caviar trade, transferring the money they earned to their village. The Church of Saints Constantine and Helena and the Şakir Paşa Madrasa in the center of the village, the Saint Nicholas Church and its monastery near the village, along with the many superb mansions, contribute a very special atmosphere to the village. The doors of the historical homes display an even more distinctive beauty.

Below, a view from the Mustafapaşa.

Opposite page, houses of the authentic masonry tradition offer magnificient views in Mustafapaşa.

'Little Ihlara', in the Gömede Valley

Between Ürgüp and Mustafapaşa Köyü, approximately two kilometers from Mustafapaşa, lies the Gömede Valley, like a small copy of the Ihlara Valley. Monasteries and churches where in the past the monks lived their monastic lives are to be found here. Among these churches, the most important is the Church of Saint Basileios, carved into the tuff rock of a hilltop in the valley. This pre-Iconoclatic Era church with two apses, two naves, and a rectangular shape, contains on the full length of its ceiling a large fresco of a cross ornamented with vegetal and geometric motifs. Its walls are decorated in red earth dye with the motifs of the Iconoclastic Era; the door that opens toward the Gömede Valley is in ruins. Above the east apse are three Maltese crosses and decorations with plant motifs. Two figures in the apse represent Saint Basileios of Caesarea and Saint Gregory of Nazianzos. An inscription that extends the full length of the wall mentions the name of the Byzantine Emperor Constantine, who was canonized a saint.

Right, the cross form which extends all along the vault of the Gömede Church of Saint Basileios.

Opposite page, churches and dovecotes in Gömede Valley.

Ottoman structures of Taşkınpaşa Köyü

On the road from Ürgüp to Soğanlı, just past Mustafapaşa Köyü, is Taşkınpaşa Köyü, a village named for a general of the IIkhanid Era. The commander Taşkın Paşa was born and raised in this village, and is buried in the cupola-shaped tomb adjacent to the mosque he commissioned here. The Taşkınpaşa Mosque contained a walnut pulpit and a *mihrab* (the niche designating the direction of the kiblah) that is the only example of its kind, both of which are on display at the Ankara Ethnographic Museum. The *mihrab* is a masterpiece of art carved with verses from the Qur'an and geometric designs. The columns inside the mosque are works from the Early Byzantine Era, and were brought to Taşkınpaşa from the antique settlement of Sobessos, which is not far away.

Opposite page, below and right, the wooden *mihrab* of Taşkınpaşa Mosque, preserved in the Museum of Ethnography, Ankara.

Below left, Taşkınpaşa Mosque and Tomb.

Şahinefendi Köyü, site of the antique city of Sobessos

Along the Ürgüp-Soğanlı road, approximately 12 kilometers south of Ürgüp, you will find the village of Şahinefendi, a home to fascinating fairy chimneys and rock churches. But most importantly, the remains of the ancient city of Sobessos, whose archaeological excavation is ongoing, are located within the limits of this village. Among the rock-hewn churches in the vicinity of the village is the one known as Kırk Şehitler [Forty Martyrs], which contains a fresco on the topic of the Forty Martyrs of Sebasteia (Sivas) that is the best interpretation in Cappadocia. This composition portrays the martyrdom of the forty by Roman soldiers during the early years of Christianity.

the outer view of Kırkşehitler Church, in the vicinity of Şahinefendi Village of Ürküp.

The antique city of Sobessos, a new discovery

Located within the limits of Şahinefendi Köyü, the ancient city of Sobessos is one of the most significant archaeological discoveries in the Cappadocia region in recent years. Discoveries from the late Roman Era uncovered during the excavation being conducted since 2002 by the Nevşehir Museum consist of residences, cloakroom (*apidoterium*), warm chamber (*tepidarium*) and hot chamber (*caldarium*) of a cloverleaf-shaped bath, a 400-square meter meeting room whose flooring is partially covered with mosaic, an Early Byzantine Era chapel and graves belonging primarily to members of the clergy.

Among the multicolored mosaics that have been brought to light, geometric motifs such as the meander, swastika and braids can be viewed. The intriguing mosaic with a sandal motif on floor of the entrance to the baths adds a unique touch to the mosaic discoveries at Sobessos.

Below, the bath in the antique city of Sobessos.

Pages 114-115, detail from the scene of Forty Martyrs of Sebasteia (Sıvas) in Kırkşehitler Church in Şahinefendi Village.

STEP-BY-STEP CAPPADOCIA **FROM ÜRGÜP TO SOĞANLI**

Soğanlı, the village of handmade cloth dolls

Until about fifty years ago, Soğanlı Köyü was one of the places infrequently visited by tourists in Cappadocia. It was 'discovered' in the early 1970s, and quickly became a rather well-known destination.

Apart from its natural beauty and rich history, what has actually made Soğanlı famous are the handmade cloth dolls that are well recognized by doll collectors the world over. During the winter months when the women are forced to remain indoors, they make cloth dolls out of ever-present cloth remnants, twigs and other waste materials and save them up to sell to the tourists. It is possible to see in every rag doll the silhouette of a young girl from Soğanlı.

If you visit the village by car, park it in the village square when you arrive, because you will begin your Soğanlı tour from this square.

Soğanlı Village with its natural beauty.

SOĞANLI'S UNIQUE CHURCHES

The naive frescoes of the Karabaş Kilisesi

A few hundred meters from the Soğanlı Köyü square you will arrive at Karabaş Kilisesi, perched on a high point in the valley. The church was named 'Karabaş' [meaning 'dark head'] because the head of each individual in the frescoes has been painted in dark colors, from Jesus to the saints, and Mary to Joseph. The walls of the church display naively executed compositions of the Nativity, Presentation at the Temple, Resurrection and Annunciation. It appears that part of Karabaş Kilisesi was used as a monastery, and under the crumbling plaster of this section, which was previously part of the church, can be seen traces of frescoes in lighter colors.

Above left, Resurrection (Anastasis), Karabaş Church.

Below left, Presentation at the Temple, Karabaş Church.

A chateau-like structure, Kubbeli Kilise

It is very pleasant to view Kubbeli Kilise [Domed Church] across the valley from the natural terrace of the Karabaş Kilisesi. Reminiscent of a chateau when seen from a distance, this church was also constructed during the Byzantine Era. It can be reached by a twenty-minute walk from the Karabaş Kilisesi, down a footpath from the asphalt road. The scenery becomes even more beautiful as you walk and climb the hill. The tuff outside the tuff mass in which it is carved is also carved to form which looks like a stone structure.

Kubbeli Church looks like a castle from a distance.

Tahtalı Kilise [Church of Saint Barbara], among the trees

On the west side of the Soğanlı Valley among apricot trees you will find the Tahtalı Kilise, which dates to the tenth century. Most of the frescoes decorating the apse and walls of this single nave, barrel-vaulted church are representations of saints. In addition, like in many archaic Cappadocian churches, a "narrative cycle" which depicts the life of Jesus with a series of frescoes with scenes like The Nativity, Three Wise Kings is displayed here. A large number of hermit cells surrounding the church is also noteworthy.

Resurrection (*Anastasis*), Tahtalı Church (The Church of Saint Barbara).

FROM AKSARAY TO IHLARA

Historical riches of Aksaray

On the road to Ihlara from Aksaray one is sure to meet numerous natural and architectural riches worth of seeing. Dominating the landscape and rising to a height of 3,268 meters Mount Hasan is the second-highest peak in Central Anatolia, and is located approximately 30 km from the province of Aksaray. The mountain that is now covered up to 1,750 meters with oak forests is a volcano that was extinguished many centuries ago. Hasan Dağı is extremely rich from the standpoint of its cultural wealth. The Kale and Sarıgöl churches at Yenipınar, the antique city of Makissos (Viranşehir) near Helvadere, the Tepe, Yardıbaş and Süt churches, and the Çukurpınar church at Dedesivri are the first historical treasures in the near vicinity of the mountain that come to mind. With Selime Village, Ihlara and Güzelyurt further on the route, Aksaray forms a triange, with its location at the top. The natural wonders of the Ihlara Valley, Belisırma and Yaprakhisar rest within this triangle.

Aksaray is a district center located 60 km west of Nevşehir along the Ankara-Konya highway. Known as Archelaus in the Antique Era, it was named for the last king of Cappadocia, Archelaos. An important settlement in Byzantine as well as Seljuk times, Aksaray hosts numerous caravanserai, mosque, fountain and tombs dating the the Seljuk and Ottoman eras. The caravanserais of Sultanhan and Ağzıkarahan are undoubtedly the largest and most important in Anatolia. The newly renovated and opened Aksaray Museum is renowned for the Byzantine-era mummies discovered in the region. This museum exhibiting lovely and fascinating objects from the Prehistoric, Hittite, Phrygian, Roman and Byzantine eras is one of the spots that should be on your 'must see' list.

Opposite page, Mount Hasan, 30 kilometers from Aksaray.

Moslem-Christian Saint Mamas in Gökçe Village

On the road from Nevşehir towards Aksaray, just a few kilometers before the Ağzıkarahan Caravanserai, the road turning off to the left will take you to Gökçe Köyü. One of the smallest villages in the region, Gökçe is home to the tomb of the Christian Saint Mamas, which is today accepted as a Moslem burial place. This grave which was transformed by the people of the region into a Moslem tomb is situated within a Byzantine church that dates to the fifth to sixth century. According to legend and hearsay, Saint Mamas was a young shepherd who was born and raised here, but because he was a fervent Christian who spread Christianity to those around him, he was taken to Kayseri [Caesarea] and martyred by torture; a few centuries later his body was returned to the village of his birth for burial.

Saint Mamas Tomb, Gökçe Village.

Ağzıkarahan Caravanserai, built by Keyhüsrev

Along the route from Nevşehir to Aksaray, about 15 km from Aksaray, is the Ağzıkarahan Caravanserai, whose construction was begun in 1231 by the Seljuk Sultan Alaeddin Keykubad and completed by his son Gıyaseddin Keyhusrev. One of the most beautiful caravanserais in Central Anatolia, in addition to its summer and winter quarters, it has a small mosque in the courtyard that is still in very good condition today.

The ornamented portal of Ağzıkarahan, one of the most beautiful caravanserais of Central Anatolia.

Sultanhan, with its beautiful portal

Sultanhan is located about 40 km to the southwest of Aksaray on the road between Ankara and Konya. The entry gate of this caravanserai constructed in 1228 by the Seljuk Sultan Alaeddin Keykubad is one of the most beautiful examples of portals of its era. It has a small mosque in the center of its courtyard and consists of summer and winter quarters. A cupola-shaped conical dome typical of the Seljuk Era rises above its large winter quarters.

Left, the small mosque in the courtyard of Sultanhan, on the road between Konya-Aksaray.

Below, the impressive portal of Sultanhan.

Güzelyurt, cradle of monastic life

Güzelyurt is 45 km east of Aksaray, 15 km northeast of the Ihlara Valley; it is approximately 40 km from the Derinkuyu underground city via the recently constructed new road. Known during the Roman and Byzantine eras as Kalvari, during the Ottoman era it was called Gelveri.

Of the most important Greek Orthodox ecclesiastics, Basileios was from Caesarea/Kayseri and Gregory was from Kalveri/Güzelyurt. The very first monastery in the region began its life in Güzelyurt. Even during the most powerful days of the Iconoclasm movement, the region provided an important shelter for Christian religious functionaries.

Güzelyurt was founded on hard rocky ground 1,500 meters above sea level near Hasan Dağı. The town is adorned with beautiful examples of Greek houses made of quarried stone. Constructed with large blocks of cut stone because of the cold climate, most of the houses bear the name of the owner, the year of construction and a prayer. Here you can also visit the hot springs of Ilısu Village and the ruins of Helvadere/Mokissos.

Güzelyurt is divided into three sections: the Yeni [New], Aşağı [Lower] and Yukarı [Upper] Mahalle [neighborhoods].

GÜZELYURT'S IMPRESSIVE STRUCTURES

Bucak Kilisesi, for those seeking health

In the town's upper section, the Yukarı Mahalle, the church of St. Anargiros, Sivişli, or the Bucak Church as it is otherwise known, is partly hewn into the rock, while its façade consists of layered stone. The church is built in the shape of a Greek cross; because its inscription is missing, the date of construction cannot be known for certain, but it is believed that the church was built between the ninth and twelfth centuries. The church underwent repairs in 1884, and its frescoes were painted in 1887. On the 1st of November, the feast day of Saint Anargiros, special ceremonies were held, and sick people seeking cures for their ills were brought here especially for these feast days.

Aziz Gregory Kilisesi, transformed into a mosque

Located in the Aşağı Mahalle, the Saint Gregory Church was the town's most important church until the population exchanges of 1924. Because the inscription of this church in the shape of a Greek cross is lost, the date of construction is not known for certain. However, it has been suggested that the initial church was constructed in the fourth century. The church is said to have been commissioned in the year 385 by Saint Gregory with the financial support of the Emperor Theodosius. After the Orthodox Greeks left the region in1924, the church was transformed into a mosque and renamed the Büyük Kilise Camii [The Mosque of the Great Church].

The main area of worship is covered by a high dome resting on eight tambours. The protruding apse is covered by a semidome. The bell tower, whose bells are said to have been heard up to three hours away on days of worship, was later transformed into a minaret. There is also a holy spring in the garden of the church. The icons, lamps and other valuable furnishings of the church are said to have been transported by the departing Greeks to the Saint Gregory Church in their new settlement of Nea Kalvari near Kavala, Greece.

The Great Church
Mosque, Güzelyurt.

Interconnected underground cities

There are five interconnected underground cities beneath
Güzelyurt. The entrance to the largest and most important
of them is on Cevizli Sokak. The interconnected cities have
square floor plans and small rooms, with narrow tunnels that
descend at an angle of 45 degrees.

Kaya Cami, carved into the rock

A part of the Kaya Mescit or Kaya Mosque is carved into the
rock, and was the most important place of worship for the
Moslems who lived here during the Ottoman Era. Believed
to have been constructed in the fourteenth century, it has lost
its authentic condition at the present time, but is noteworthy
for its mihrab, which was carved into the rock.

Yüksek Kilise [Saint Mamas Monastery] on the heights

On the Analipsis Tepesi [Peak] across from Güzelyurt is the
nineteenth-century Yüksek Kilise, otherwise known as the
Saint Mamas Monastery. At one time the Christians in the region used to celebrate their feast days around this monastery
built of grey and black volcanic rock. Traces of prehistoric settlements have been found in the vicinity of the hill, and the
small pond formed by accumulated rainwater gives the hill the
appearance of a pleasant island.

Manastırlar Vadisi [Valley of Monasteries] surrounded by rock

Located near Güzelyurt, with a river running down the center of its 5.5-kilometer length, is Manastırlar Vadisi, the Valley of Monasteries, surrounded on both sides by high rock
formations. In the valley surrounded by willows and with a
river in the middle there are approximately fifty churches and
monasteries, but the frescoes are in rather bad condition.

Kızıl Kilise, a World Heritage site

Also known as the Church of Saint Spiridon, the Kızıl Kilise [The Red Church] in the Göller Bölgesi can be reached by a 45-minute walk. Constructed in 1084, the church's two symmetrical naves are in poor condition. The church has been placed on the World Heritage List because of its powerful design, its rarely used reddish stones and because it is in rather good condition; it takes its name from the reddish quarried stone used in its construction.

The Church of Saint Spiridon (Kızıl Kilise) takes its name from the reddish quarried stones used in its construction.

Ihlara Vadisi [Valley], a magnificent canyon

From Aksaray take the Nevşehir asphalt for 11 km and you will see on your right the turnoff for the Ihlara Vadisi. The valley is actually approximately 33 km. from Aksaray. Also known as the Peristrema Valley, the Ihlara Valley continues through Belisırma and Yaprakhisar and ends at Selime Köyü. Ihlara can also be reached via Niğde and Derinkuyu. Four kilometers of the 14km-long valley are easy to see and tour.

During the tertiary geological era, the tectonic movement that caused the eruptions of Mount Erciyes in the east and Hasan Dağı in the west resulted in the surface of the region being covered with a volcanic layer. While the mixture of different types of lava created rolling plains, the hard lava layers at their outskirts with dense concentrations of andesite and basalt eventually were transformed into layers of volcanic tuff and limestone. In addition to the effects of natural phenomena such as rain, snow and wind, the Melendiz Çayı's [Stream] erosion of this lava over millions of years eventually caused the formation of the long, deep Ihlara Valley, which has the appearance of a canyon, surrounded as it is by 100-150 meter-high rocks and steep cliffs. The Melendiz Çayı, winding its way along the cracks it had eroded, was

Below and opposite page, the River Melendiz carved the tuff rock and formed the almost-hidden valley, which can not be seen unless approached closely. The part of the valley where Melendiz runs through between Selime and Ihlara villages is known as the Ihlara Valley.

originally named Potamus Kapadukus, meaning Cappadocia River. After passing through Ihlara, the Melendiz Çayı passes through Belisırma, and near Aksaray takes the name Ulu Irmak [meaning 'great river] before flowing into Tuz Gölü, 'Salt Lake'.

During the tectonic movements mentioned above, naturally hot water sprang through the broken faultlines to form the Ziga Kaplıcaları [thermal springs] located between Yaprakhisar and Ihlara. The surroundings of Selime Köyü are filled with fairy chimneys of different shapes and colors.

Considered one of the world's most important and beautiful canyons, the Ihlara Canyon, together with the Valla and Kara Cehennem canyons in Kastamonu, the Çoruh Valley, the Eşen, Köprülü, Saklıkent and Güver canyons of Antalya and the Lamas and Mut canyons of Mersin, are among Turkey's major canyons. Before beginning to tour the Ihlara Valley, take a look at the general panorama from the sightseeing terrace. Listen to the birdsong coming from the incredibly beautiful emerald-green trees. Then descend the roughly 400 steps to start your tour in the direction of the flowing water among the acacia, willow, pistachio, nettleberry, poplar, almond and walnut trees and bushes of rosehips.

The characteristic geography and strategic location of the Ihlara Valley provided an appropriate location for clerics and monastics for worship and seclusion from the earliest years of Christianity. In the fourth century Saint Basileios and Saint Gregory established the regulations for a form of religious life different from that practiced in Egypt and Syria; this was the cenobitic, or community form, of monastic life which did not rest on cutting off all ties with the world. This new concept flourished in Belisirma and was widely imitated, later giving birth to the Greek and Slavic systems that were an alternative to the monastery systems of Egypt and Syria.

Known to be born in 329, Saint Gregory became a leading Christian saint in large part because of the different interpretation he made of the Holy Trinity accepted at the Council of Nicea (present-day İznik) which had taken place in 325. At this famous council, the true divinity of Christ as Son of God and the four Bibles were affirmed.

In later eras the churches carved from the rock would

appear in Güzelyurt, Belisırma and Ihlara. In some cases the churches and monasteries were connected by tunnels. Even during the era of Arab invasions the well-hidden churches in the valleys continued to function. The frescoes in the churches of the Ihlara Valley are dated to different periods, from the sixth through the thirteenth centuries.

While the wall paintings in the churches close to the Ihlara Valley are somewhat remote from Cappadocian art, with a visible Oriental influence, the churches close to Belisırma show a marked Byzantine influence. In the churches that were generally constructed in three storeys, the first levels have been filled with alluvial deposits carried by the Melendiz Stream. Of the churches that are in a condition to be toured, it is generally their second and third storeys that can be viewed. Of the 105 churches that include those that have been demolished or buried in debris, the number of churches still standing is only about fifteen.

A view from the Ihlara Valley.

HIDDEN CHURCHES IN IHLARA

At the valley's entrance, Ağaçaltı Kilisesi [Church of Daniel Pantanassa]

Descending to the Ihlara Valley, the first church seen by visitors is the Ağaçaltı Kilisesi, below and to the right. It has a cruciform floor plan and a single dome. The arms of the cross are covered with barrel vaulting that is decorated with vegetal and geometric motifs. The church has been dated to the ninth to eleventh centuries. Of its three apses only one remains standing.

The church is entered through the demolished main apse. In the decorations, the colors red, grey and yellow predominate on a white ground. The Ascension of Jesus to Heaven is depicted on the dome, along with pictures of saints. The Annunciation, Flight into Egypt, Baptism, Assumption of Mary into Heaven, Three Wise Kings, and Daniel in the Lions' Den are among the principal topics of the church's frescoes. The composition of the Three Wise Kings displays a distinctive difference from the frescoes of the same name in the churches of Cappadocia: here the three wise kings have an appearance reminiscent of Mevlevi dervishes.

Opposite page,
Ağaçaltı Church, Ihlara.

Eğritaş Kilise [Panagia Church], dedicated to Mary

Dating to the late ninth to early tenth centuries, according to its inscription the Eğritaş Kilise is dedicated to the Mother Mary. The church has a single nave and barrel vaulting, and at the side there is section that is connected to burial chambers. The frescoes on its walls contain scenes from the Bible. One of the more interesting frescoes is the Dream of the Wise Kings, a topic that is rarely seen in the Cappadocia frescoes. In the arched section, Jesus is portrayed between two angels. Although the scenes of the Flight into Egypt and Entry into Jerusalem along with the frescoes of angels, apostles and Saints Gregory and Basileios are quite time-worn, they are still in a distinguisable condition.

Kokar Kilise, with its grey frescoes

The church dates to the ninth to eleventh century, and it is one of the churches whose frescoes can be considered in good condition. The entry to the single-nave, barrel-vaulted church is through its collapsed apse. The color grey predominates in its frescoes.

The vault is decorated with a large cross. Among the familiar fresco compositions of the *Deisis*, Annunciation, Visitation, Nativity, Respects of the Wise Kings, Flight into Egypt, Crucifixion, Burial, Women before the Empty Sepulchre and Ascension, there are scenes not often found in the Cappadocia churches, such as the Trial by Water and the Three Jewish Youths thrown into the Burning Furnace. In another composition, Mary is depicted between the archangels Michael and Gabriel. In addition to the saints, prophet-kings such as David and Solomon are also portrayed here.

**Opposite page,
Kokar Church.**

Pürenli Seki Kilise, with four sections

Consisting of four sections carved out of the rock, the Pürenli Church is dated to the tenth to twelfth centuries, and takes its name from the *püren otu*, a species of heath that grows abundantly in the vicinity. Burial niches are visible in the narthex of the cruciform church. The most interesting of the church's wall paintings is the depiction of the angels Michael, Gabriel, Raphael and Azrael flying through grey clouds bearing Jesus. Among the other important frescoes in the church are the Oracles of the Prophets, Mary and the Bishops, Annunciation, Visitation, Worshipping Shepherds, Last Judgment, Entry into Jerusalem, Last Supper, Crucifixion, Ascension, Daniel in the Lion's Den and Christian Martyrs.

Sümbüllü Kilise and its rare frescoes

One of the churches constructed in the Ihlara Valley during the era following the Byzantine recapture of the Cilicia region is the Sümbüllü Church [Narcissus Church]. The cruciform church was carved into a huge rock mass, and its first level was left in the form of a cave. There are four columns, two doors and three blind windows on the second floor. The eleventh and twelfth-century frescoes in the church display characteristics not encountered in other Cappadocia churches. On the dome is the Pantocrator Christ and saints, with Saint Gregory and Saint Theodoros portrayed within medallions. In addition to the depiction of four important holydays, the Annunciation, the Presentation at the Temple, the Crucifixion and the Ascension, other important frescoes consist of Mary among the Angels and the Three Jewish Youths thrown into the Burning Furnace.

Opposite page, the facade of Sümbüllü Church.

Below, Pantocrator Christ on the dome of Sümbüllü Church.

Yılanlı Kilise and its frescoes of serpents

The church dates to the tenth to eleventh century, and belongs to the group of cruciform churches; it is covered with barrel-vaulting. The church was constructed by monks who had fled from the Arabs and taken refuge in the region. It is one of the churches whose frescoes have remained in good condition. There are graves in the north wall.

One of the church's most beautiful frescoes is the scene of the Archangel Michael Weighing Sins. It is because of the depiction on the west wall of Four Sinful Women whose bodies are enwrapped by serpents that the church is called the 'Church of Serpents'. The inscription area on the fresco is partially erased, so we do not know the sin of the first woman. The serpents have bitten the second woman on the breast because she did not suckle her child, the third woman on the tongue because she lied, and the fourth woman on the ears because she was disobedient and recalcitrant. Angels and scenes from the life of Jesus can be seen on the arches. Topics of other frescoes include the Ascension, the Last Judgment, the Last Supper, the Crucifixion and the Entry into Jerusalem.

Opposite page and below, depictions of saints in Yılanlı Church.

Renowned inscription in Kırkdamaltı Kilise
[Church of Saint George]

One of the few Byzantine-era inscriptions that has remained intact in the Ihlara Valley is to be found in the Kırkdamaltı Kilise. This inscription is the best proof of the liberal administration of the Seljuk state. From the second half of the tenth century the Byzantine Empire had recognized the Islamic mystic saints of Khorasan. This would become an important step for tolerance between religions. In the inscription above the niche on the north wall of the church, the Seljuk Sultan Mesud II and the Byzantine Emperor Andronikos II are praised highly.

Below, a detail from the fresco depicting Saint George and Theodore on horseback battling the dragon, Kırkdamaltı Church, Ihlara.

Opposite page, the benefactor of the church, Thamar has the model of the church in her hand, Kırkdamaltı Church.

Located 500 meters from the village of Belisırma, the Kırkdamaltı Kilise has a hexagonal shape and is the highest church in the valley. Constructed between 1283 and 1295, it is one of the few churches whose date of construction is known for certain, and is also one of the churches with the best-preserved frescoes in the Ihlara Valley. One of the rare and fascinating scenes that is rarely seen in frescoes is the Murder of Zechariah. The church also contains frescoes of Biblical themes such as the Nativity and the Death of Mary, along with portrayals of the saints.

BYZANTINE-INFLUENCED CHURCHES OF BELISIRMA

Direkli Kilise [Church of Columns] and its six columns

Constructed between the years 976 and 1025, this is another of the rare churches whose construction date is known. The cruciform church has three apses. The central dome is supported by six columns, for which the church has been named (*direk* meaning column in Turkish). Within the church can be found the cells in which the monks lived, as well as burial niches. The wall paintings consist of depictions of saints and angels, along with Biblical scenes.

Right, in Direkli Church thick piers are used instead of thin columns.

Opposite page, pictures of saints in Direkli Church.

Bahattin Samanlığı Kilisesi, named for its discoverer

Appoximately 50 meters from the Direkli Kilise is the church
discovered by a villager named Bahattin, who had used it
as a hayloft (*samanlık*) until 1950; the name has remained.
The church dates to the tenth to eleventh centuries. Domed,
with barrel vaulting and a single nave, the side walls contain
cells carved into the rock. Its frescoes remain in good condi-
ton: among them is the one painted on the dome depicting
Christ seated on a throne and next to Him, medallions depicting the archangels Michael and Gabriel and Saints Peter
and Paul. Other frescoes include the Dream of Joseph, the
Journey to Bethlehem, the Nativity, Three Wise Kings, The
Decree of the Roman governor to Kill the Children, the
Presentation at the Temple, the Baptism, Raising of Lazarus
from the Dead, the Entry into Jerusalem, the Last Supper
and the Crucifixion.

Ala Kilise, a former linseed oil press

One of the monastery churches that exemplifies eleventh-
century Byzantine art in Belissırma is the Ala Kilise. After
leaving the Bahattin Samanlığı Kilisesi, cross the Melendiz
Stream via the bridge and climb the slope leading to the left
to reach the Ala Kilise. At one time the villagers used this
building to process flax seed for its oil, and the furnace, stone
press and reservoir are still in place. The former residents of
Belisırma would squeeze the flax with a screw press between
layers of straw, and use the linseed oil it produced for oil lamps
and night lights.

The main entrance to the church has a round arch
and there are small arched entrances on either side. The main
facade presents a lively appearance, with rectangular columns
and blind windows. Unfortunately the wall paintings are not
in good condition and their color has lost its liveliness. Among
the frescoes, the Nativity, the Last Supper, the Sanctification
of Mary and the Three Jewish Youths thrown into the Burning Furnace are scenes worthy of note.

Kale Manastırı Kilisesi [Fortress Monastery Church] in Selime Village

This church is located at the other end of the Ihlara Valley in the village of Selime Köyü, and is one of Cappadocia's largest religious buildings. The monastery church is situated to surround two large courtyards. The meeting room of the monks has survived in rather good condition. The church, which dates to the eighth century, also has a kitchen, a refectory and burial chambers. The frescoes have been dated to the tenth-eleventh century. Like other churches, the topics consist of Biblical scenes.

Wheel of Torture in the Karagedik Kilise [Church of Saint Ermolaos]

The Karagedik Kilise, which has been dated to the eleventh century, is not in good condition because of the rocks that have fallen on it. Built of quarried stone, the cruciform church with four columns also has a dome with pendentives. Because its frescoes have been partially erased, they are not clearly visible. On the arches there are representations of the saints and in one corner, an interesting composition with a wheel of torture.

Karagedik Church is in ruins due to the fallen rocks over it.

FROM NEVŞEHİR TO HACIBEKTAŞ

Nevşehir, city at the center of Cappadocia

Known as Nyssa in ancient times, Nevşehir is one of the five large districts of the Cappadocia region along with Kayseri, Kırşehir, Niğde and Aksaray, and is located in the center of the world of fairy chimneys. A settlement of only eighteen homes named Muşkara during early Ottoman times, the town was named Nevşehir during the reign of Sultan Ahmet III after his son-in-law Nevşehirli İbrahim Paşa, and grew rapidly within a short time by means of a large series of public works to become a city of importance.

The Kurşunlu Cami, famous for its carvings

Below, *kalemişleri* in the dome of Kurşunlu Mosque.

Opposite page, Kurşunlu Mosque, Nevşehir.

Built on the outskirts of the Seljuk-era Nevşehir Fortress in 1726, the Kurşunlu Cami [Leaded Mosque], was constructed as a part of Nevşehirli İbrahim Paşa's complex of buildings. It takes its name from the lead covering of its dome, and is a typical Ottoman mosque. The interior of the mosque provides a dazzling display of painted floral decoration, and the mosque itself is surrounded by the baths, library, madrasah and public kitchen that complete the complex.

Nevşehir Museum, the history of Cappadocia

Nevşehir is home to a small but beautiful museum that reflects the long history of the region, from the Prehistoric Era through the Roman, Byzantine and Ottoman Eras. Divided into two sections, archaeological and ethnographic, the museum exhibits items discovered in Cappadocia as diverse as fossils of prehistoric animals like the mammoth, Neolithic pottery, finds from Roman graves and coins from different eras. In addition to this selection, you can view ethnographic items of daily use by the people of the region, from carpets to costumes.

The renowned Avanos Sarcophagus displayed in the garden of the museum is one of the most attractive pieces in the collection.

Η ΝΕΑΠΟΛΙΣ ΙΚΟΝΙΟΥ ΝΕΒ.ΣΕΧΙΡ

Above, two-handled jar,
terracotta, finding from
Civelek Cave, Nevşehir
Museum.

Left, a lithograph of
Nevşehir, executed in
latter 19th. century,
Nevşehir Museum.

Gülşehir, with beautiful Ottoman structures

Located 20 kilometers from Nevşehir, Gülşehir is the continuation of the ancient settlement of Zoropassos, which was later renamed Arapsun. After Nevşehir, it was the second Cappadocian town to provide the Ottoman State with a grand vizier. Karavezir Mehmet Seyyid Paşa was born here, and after accepting the duties of a state dignitary, revitalized the village of his birth by donating a mosque, madrasah, library and fountains. Gülşehir lies south of the Kızılırmak riverbed, and in addition to the Mehmet Seyyid Paşa Mosque in its town center, has a number of other very important and beautiful historical locales in its vicinity.

Mantar Kaya, symbol of the Açıksaray ruins

Three kilometers from Gülşehir in the direction of Nevşehir are the Açıksaray ruins, home to structures carved into the rocks in Roman and Byzantine times as well as fascinating fairy chimneys. A bishopric during the Byzantine Era, Gülşehir also boasts the presence of a small square mosque named for Hacı Bektaş Veli dating to the Seljuk Era, the ninth to tenth century, proof that in addition to the Christian monks, it also had a sizeable Muslim population. One of the 'must see' sights in this area is Mantar Kaya [Mushroom Rock], a fairy chimney whose beauty and size is unrivalled. The mushroom shape that the winds have formed of its layers has almost become the symbol of Açıksaray.

Opposite page, Mantar Kaya in Açıksaray ruin.

Karşı Kilise [Church of Saint John], with its unique frescoes

Below, Saint George and Saint Theodore on horseback battling the dragon, Karşı Church, Gülşehir.

Opposite page, above left, Judas's Betrayal. Above right, Hell in the Last Judgement scene. Middle left, Baptism. Middle right, two Marys at the Grave. Below left, Resurrection (*Anastasis*). Below right, Weighing of Souls in the Last Judgement.

This two-storey church at the entrance to the Açıksaray ruins is one of the most beautiful in Cappadocia. The artist or group of artists who produced the wall paintings here have painted frescoes whose lines and colors are in a school of their own. The frescoes were painstakingly restored in 1995 in a manner that will preserve them safely for the future. The walls of the upper storey of the church are covered with frescoes from end to end portraying one scene from the Bible after another. The barrel-vaulted church bears on its apse the number 1212, an indication that the frescoes were most likely produced in the twelfth and thirteenth centuries. Among the compositions which are, in general, on a dark-colored background, are the *Deisis* (Supplication), the Annunciation, the Last Supper, Judas's Betrayal, the Baptism of Christ, the Death of Mary, the Descent of Jesus from the Cross, the Women Weeping in front of the Empty Grave, the Resurrection and the Last Judgment.

Hacıbektaş District, center of Bektashism

The district of Hacıbektaş is located approximately 45 kilometers along the road from Nevşehir to Kırşehir, and is named for the great philosopher, mystic and founder of Bektashism, Hacı Bektaş Veli, who was born in the thirteenth century in Khorasan, Iran, and came here during the years that the Seljuk Empire was being established in Anatolia. A staunch defender of Islamic philosophy and Turkish unity, Hacı Bektaş Veli settled in the Suluca Karahöyük village, gathering around him youths whom he taught and inspired with pure Turkish and Turkish culture; his life style, rectitude and good deeds won him the love and respect, not only of the Muslims, but of the Christians of the region as well.

Hacı Bektaş Veli Museum, traces of Bektashism

The Hacı Bektaş Veli Türbesi ve Dergâhı [Tomb and Dervish Lodge] constructed in 1519 is a large complex consisting of a mosque, guesthouse, laundry room, kitchen and fountains, and today functions as a museum. The Dervish Lodge consists of three interconnected courtyards [avlu] and the buildings within them.

Known as the Nadar Avlusu, the first courtyard contains a fountain dating to 1902, a Turkish bath and a laundry room.

Known as the Dergâh Avlusu, or lodge courtyard, the second courtyard is entered through the famous gate [kapı] known as Üçler Kapısı. To the right of this entrance is a fountain dating to 1554, known as the Aslanlı Çeşme [Fountain with Lion]. The marble statuette of a lion was sent there by the

Hacı Bektaş Veli Tomb and Dervish Lodge, built in 1519.

daughter of the governor of Egypt, Kavalalı Mehmet Ali Paşa, in 1875. The mosque in this courtyard was commissioned by Sultan Mahmud II, along with the lodge and the guesthouse. The kitchen and larders are in the same courtyard.

Known as the Hazret Avlusu, the third courtyard is entered via the Altılar Kapısı. In the section resembling a large garden that is called the Kırklar Meydanı are the cupola-shaped tombs and graves of Bektashi dervishes. The most important and most imposing of these is the tomb of Hacı Bektaş Veli, which is a site of frequent pilgrimage. Constructed by Sultan Orhan, the second sultan of the Ottoman State, the tomb bears the characteristics of Seljuk architecture. Inside the structure containing the tomb, or *türbe*, you will also find the museum of the Hacı Bektaş Veli Lodge. The museum exhibits include Bektashi standards, printed scarves, the Bektashi vessels known as *keşkül*, and various objects used in the lodge's rites. There is also a small *çilehane* [a small dark room used for meditation].

To the east of the Kırklar Meydanı are the graves of Khorasan soldiers, and to the west, the Güvenç Abdal Türbesi and the graves of dervishes. On the right-hand side of the Hazret Avlusu you will also see the Balım Sultan Türbesi, constructed in 1519.

The Fountain with Lion in Hacı Bektaş Veli complex.

FURTHER READING

Dovecotes

When you turn off the Nevşehir-Ürgüp highway towards Uçhisar, as you approach the town center you will see off to your right both a view of a spectacular valley and one of Cappadocia's most distinctive features, the dovecotes. These homes for doves that can sometimes be seen above the fairy chimneys and sometimes in the upper sections of the valley are visions that multiply the beauty of Cappadocia. In mythology the dove was one of the symbols of Aphrodite, goddess of beauty and love, and this bird also has a special place in all the sacred books. In the Torah, the story of Noah's Ark relates that, after the Flood, Noah released a dove in an attempt to learn whether they were approaching land, and that it returned with an olive branch in its beak. In the New Testament, when Jesus is baptized by John the Baptist, the Holy Spirit in the form of a white dove alights on His head. The dove is the symbol of the Holy Spirit in the Christian doc-

Chimneys converted into dovecotes in Uçhisar region.

trine of the Holy Trinity. In the Qur'an the Prophet Moham-
med, while fleeing from the Kureyshis, finds refuge in a cave
whose entry is immediately covered over by a web spun by
spiders and where a dove has nested in order to safeguard the
Prophet. In short, the dove is considered sacred in all three
Abrahamic traditions.

From the sixteenth century onward, one finds bird-
houses for doves in Anatolian mosques and in civil architecture. Most Moslems consider doves sacred, and neither hunt
them nor eat their flesh (except in Egypt). There have been
dovecotes in Cappadocia since the Byzantine era. The entrances to the dovecotes have been decorated with colorful
designs since the nineteenth century.

In the Cappadocian dovecotes there are generally
three to four holes side by side or two rows of three holes
each, one above the other. The dovecote interior is on the
average 5-10m². There are nest-shaped hollows carved around
the edges for the birds to lay their eggs, and wooden perches
have been placed in them. Even the smallest of the dovecotes
can accommodate more than one hundred doves. The dovecotes have been situated at rather high spots in the valleys, and
can only be reached by a narrow tunnel from the inside or

**examples from the
facade ornamentations
of dovecotes.**

via a monopod ladder. Most of the dovecotes in Cappadocia are to be found in the Ürgüp Üzengi Valley, the Soğanlı Valley and the vicinity of Uçhisar. These dovecotes have been carved out of the tuff rock, and like homes for people, these 'homes' were created specifically for the doves. The most beautiful examples of this type of dovecote can be seen at the Çavuşin churches, the Göreme Kılıçlar Church and the Ortahisar Hallaç Monastery.

However, the most important reason for the presence of so many dovecotes in Cappadocia is not the beauty or sacred status of the birds, but the use of their manure as fertilizer. Bird manure is used in some parts of the world to improve the yield of crops. The fertilizer of the pigeon or dove contains 20-25% organic matter, 1-2% nitrogen and 0.5-1.5% phosphoric acid, which is extremely useful in agriculture. Cappadocians have used this fertilizer on their crops for hundreds of years, and continue to do so.

The exteriors of the dovecotes have been decorated by regional artists according to their traditions and social cus-

Opposite page, Uçhisar Castle, one of the panaromic sights of Cappadocia.

Below, dovecotes of the Çat Valley.

toms. The pigments used for decoration are derived from the rich chemistry of the region's soil. The red comes from the abundant local clay known as *yoşa*, the green from the shells and leaves of walnut, the yellow from the *çehri* plant [*rhamnus petiolaris*], dark red from dried grapes, pink from onionskins, grey from *yarpuz* [*menthapulegium*], and brown from the bark of *kızılağaç*, a type of native alder. A gloss is given to the decorations by painting them over with cow urine.

The greatest danger to the doves comes from predatory animals like weasels, foxes and martens that are able to climb into their nests. The local population have solved this problem by painting the entries to the dovecotes with a mixture of plaster and eggwhite, which makes the walls slippery, and consequently the predators are unable to reach the nests. In some locations, instead of using this mixture, the entries are blocked by nailing plaques of tin or sheet iron. Many of the dovecotes are embellished with the white paint that, as one sees in the Soğanlı Valley, pigeons seem to like. Occasionally one sees black or brown kilim motifs applied on the white surface.

On some dovecotes one can see inscriptions written in Ottoman Turkish. These inscriptions bear the dovecote's date of construction, the name of its owner and his profession. Verses from the Qur'an have been inscribed at the entrances of some of the dovecotes.

Unfortunately, with the passage of time, dovecotes too have fallen from favor. Cappadocians do not display the interest in doves that they formerly did. There is always a need for fertilizer, but it is a pity that there are few doves remaining in the dovecotes. The condition of the nesting areas is not a cheerful sight, and of course it is inevitable to feel nostalgia for the past.

Opposite page, dovecotes with their multicolour ornamented facades.

Flavors of Cappadocia

Breakfasts in Cappadocia are a very different experience: village butter, potted cheese, drained and concentrated yogurt, fresh eggs and honey in addition to the grape molasses and marmalades you can spread on hotcakes made with various fresh herbs...

The pumpkin seeds from the Nevşehir region that are consumed in generous quantities by the local population are considered the most delicious in Central Anatolia. Walnuts, almonds and apricots are among the favorites of the variety of dried fruits and nuts that adorn the table after the evening meals. And you can enjoy compotes made from the dried fruits of the region as well.

In Cappadocia you will become acquainted with all the specialties of Central Anatolian cuisine in addition to the new cuisine cultures that have been developed by the people from Turkey and other corners of the world who have come and settled here. It is a lovely surprise for foreign visitors to discover in the hotel restaurants of Cappadocia this amalgam of Turkish and world cuisine.

Cappadocia cuisine has experienced the influence of many different cultures, and foods such as wheat, dried cracked wheat, noodles and ravioli, as well as legumes such as

The collective bakery oven in Soğanlı Village.

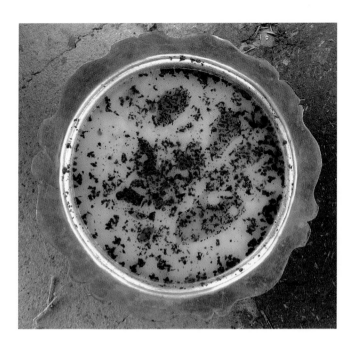

Yarma aşı which can be cold or warm eaten.

beans, chickpeas and lentils and the pita-like variety of local bread play an important role.

Fruits such as grapes, apricots, strawberries, apples, pears and quince are used both in main dishes and desserts. Pumpkin adds flavor to molasses as well as hot dishes. The grape cider that is prepared in dedicated cider rooms in the home is also very popular. Grapes and pears are arranged on thorny branches and preserved in pantries and fruitcellars for use in winter.

In old homes the tandouri oven had a number of different functions; it was used to heat the house as well as to bake bread and other foods. The old custom of slowly cooking dried beans or chickpeas with meat in an earthenware crock for about six hours is one of the first of the regional specialties that comes to mind.

Another regional speciality is yarma aşı which can be cold or warm eaten in summer.

Nevşehir mantısı.

Nevşehir Mantısı (a ravioli-like local specialty): Unlike the *mantı* we are accustomed to, the pieces of dough should be small enough to fit a few of them in a spoon. Also, they are generally served with boiled chickpeas on the side. There is also a type of meatless mantı known as *muhacir mantısı* that is made by mixing fried onions with leavened dough, and is eaten with garlic-infused yogurt poured over it.

Tıranenik: A special regional dish made with *tarhana*, (a sun-dried soup mix composed of yogurt, tomato and flour) and molasses.

Pastırmalı Börek: *Pastırma*, a type of cured spiced beef, is very well liked in this region that is so close to Kayseri, the city of pastırma. The pastırma is enfolded in a sheet of *yufka*, thin pastry dough, and fried in oil. Another special dish is humus made with pastırma.

Kıymalı sigara böreği: A savory pastry made with ground meat, it is prepared with many different spices.

Çömlek kebabı: Meat, and a variety of vegetables including potatoes, eggplant and tomatoes are cooked in an earthenware container whose top is sealed with dough. When the time comes for the dish to be served, the mouth of the crock is broken. Another specialty is *köfte* (meatballs) cooked in a sauce in an earthenware crock.

Peynirli biftek: In the Ihlara valley, a piece of beefsteak is pounded flat and grilled with a filling of regional cheese, black pepper and thyme.

Kuzu tandır and kuzu çevirme: Lamb roasted in a tandouri oven or on a spit can be found in almost every corner of the region. *Kuzu beli* is another lamb dish that is a regional specialty.

Saç tava: A large sheet-metal skillet is set over the tandouri oven, and meat cut into small pieces is sautéed along with eggplant, tomatoes, green peppers, garlic and thyme.

Ayvalı et yahnisi (meat stewed with quince): The quinces are peeled and left to soak in water with lemon juice added while onions are fried in oil. Pieces of lamb are then cooked with the onions, quince, salt, sugar and cinnamon; the dish is served with homemade noodles.

Kayısılı et yahnisi (**meat stewed with apricots**): The pieces of lamb are placed in an earthenware crock along a variety of small apricot called '*bitirgen*'; molasses is then poured over it before cooking it in the crock.

Çömlek fasulyesi: Dried beans are cooked in a crock along with lamb, tomatoes, peppers and plentiful spices.

Ermeni yahnisi: A type of stewed beans with cinnamon and onions.

Patlıcan dolması: Aubergines are stuffed with rice, onions, parsley, raisins and spices that are particular to the region. There is also a regional dish called 'tık tık' that consists of an aubergine salad.

Tavuklu yemekler, **or chicken dishes:** Chicken stuffed with spinach, walnuts and cheese; spinach and chicken in pastry; chicken with almond sauce…are just a few of the special dishes of Cappadocia cuisine.

Kora Papareni: Pastry sheets are moistened with chicken bouillon and chicken and walnuts are placed over it. It is eaten alongside another type of *börek* or savory pastry dish called '*fasulnik*'.

Deveci pilavı, **or 'camelherder pilaf':** This is a typical bulgur pilaf dish that has been made since the days when caravans passed through Anatolia. First the onions are fried and then brought to a boil with water, tomatoes, salt and pepper before the bulgur is added. It is served with garlic yogurt and flaked red pepper.

Patates köftesi: These potato rissoles are made with a variety of potato called '*kıraç*' and only made with rainwater. Some of the most flavorful potatoes in Turkey are raised in the Cappadocia region.

Çorbalar, **or soups:** Among the fascinating variety of regional soups are one called '*Düğü*' that is made with fine bulgur, chickpea soup, creamed leek soup, sesame oil soup, and carrot soup.

Boran aşı: Wheat and chickpeas are cooked together with butter, yogurt and cheese, and sprinkled with a spice called '*yarpuz*'.

Kaşıtsi: A dessert made with molasses and starch.

The rich flora of Cappadocia

Situated in the center of Anatolia between the Erciyes and Hasan Mountains, the Cappadocia region has an average elevation of 1,000 meters above sea level. Among its most predominant trees are apricot, eleagnus (*iğde*), poplar, walnut and juniper. The climate that has prevailed for centuries is ideal for growing varieties of grapes of high quality, and makes Cappadocia one of Turkey's major wine-producing centers and its vineyards an irreplaceable part of the landscape. In addition to its vineyards, the region has also been growing apples, pears and mulberries since ages past. Cappadocia is also one of Turkey's most important growing regions for potatoes and is home to the large potato farms of many manufacturers of potato chips. Like potatoes, onions and ground squash are among the region's irrevocable agricultural products.

Below left, a wildflower in Cappadocia.

Below right, apricots are cherished in the region.

Endemic species of Cappadocia fauna

Cappadocia possesses a wide range of fauna that includes endemic species. Animals such as the wolf, fox, rabbit, eagle, turtle, porcupine and ground squirrel are numerous in Cappadocia, which also harbors a rich population of butterflies. Among the endemic species of butterfly in the region is the colorful *Zygaena Kapadokia*, which holds a special place. Another endemic species to the region is the *Agama* lizard that appears on the tuff rockface in the summer, and is called '*kaya kertişi*' by the local population. This reptile with stubby spines on its tail can reach a length of 30 centimeters. The yellow scorpion, green scarabeus and horned scarabeus and insects like the potato bug are among the important living creatures in the region. Owls and different species of snakes and, in recent years, herds of wild boar complete the wealth of regional fauna.

Below left, one of the endemic species, *Zygaena Kapadokia* butterfly.

Below right, *Agama* lizard.

Lowermost left, praying mantis.

Lowermost right, horned scarabeus.

The unforgettable taste of Cappadocia wine

Cappadocia is as renowned for its vineyards and wines as it is for its fairy chimneys, and the people of the region have been involved with viniculture since ancient times. From prehistoric times to the Hittites, from the Romans to the Byzantines, wine has been considered a sacred drink attributed to the gods, and has played an important role in the Cappadocia region. Wine was also known as one of the symbols of the prophet Jesus. Decorations of bunches of grapes adorn the doors of the Üzümlü Church in the Zelve Valley and the Church of Saints Constantine and Helena in Mustafapaşa and many other places in Cappadocia.

One third of the grapes grown in Cappadocia's vineyards of tuff soil are consumed either fresh or dried to meet nutritional requirements, another third is used to make molasses and fruit juice, and the remaining third is used in winemaking. The famous white wine of Cappacodia is made from juicy Emir grapes, grown in the region since olden times. The wine is an easily drinkable, pleasant dry white wine with controlled acidity and a light green to yellow color.

The oldest and most popular type of grape in the region is the dark purple Dimrit grape, which constitutes 60% of the grapes grown in the Cappadocia region. With blending (coupage) the result is a low-acid wine without an overly high alcohol content.

Another variety of grape that has long been grown in Cappadocia is also a purple grape, known in the region by the name of Şıradar, which is similar to Kalecik Karası in both color and flavor.

In recent years there has been considerable progress in wine production, agricultural production of other native and foreign grapes has begun, and the number of prizes won in international competitions by wines of private sector production in the region have increased. Other varieties of native grapes grown in the region's vineyards include Papaz Karası, Kalecik Karası and Narince, and among foreign varieties which are undergoing growing trials are grapes like Merlot, Cabernet Sauvignon, Chardonnay and Sauvignon Blanc.

The flavor of wine in Cappadocia is something entirely different. Especially at the end of a busy day, the flavor of a wine sipped at sunset can become a beautiful memory to be cherished for years to come.

opposite page, various local and foreign grapes are cultivated in the vineyards of Cappadocia.

GLOSSARY

Glossary for church frescoes

Deisis (Intercession): One of the most important scenes to be found in many Cappadocian churches. It generally is to be found in the main apses. Jesus is in the center and is flanked by the Mother Mary and St. John the Baptist; the three are praying together for humankind.

Annunciation: In the town of Nazareth in Galilee, the Angel Gabriel visits the Virgin Mary who is engaged to marry Joseph to announce that the Holy Spirit will impregnate her and that she will bear a male child who will be named Jesus. Mary's relative, Elizabeth, the wife of Zachary, is also pregnant in spite of her advanced age. This scene depicts Mary speaking with the angel.

Visitation: After the Annunciation, Mary goes to visit Elizabeth and her husband Zachary. In frescoes depicting this visit, Mary is generally portrayed as older than Elizabeth, in spite of being younger, and the two are shown embracing.

Journey to Bethlehem: Everyone is obliged to participate in his own city in the census decreed by the Roman Emperor Augustus. Mary and Joseph leave Nazareth to travel to Bethlehem. In these scenes Mary is depicted riding a donkey and is accompanied by Joseph and a servant.

Nativity: When Mary and Joseph reach Bethlehem they are unable to find accommodation and are forced to stay in a stable, where Mary, who has reached her term, gives birth. In scenes depicting the Nativity, the 'Holy Family' of Mary, Joseph and the baby Jesus are depicted in the stable: while Mary rests, the baby Jesus is warmed by the breath of a donkey and a cow, while Joseph is in a corner, deep in thought.

Three Wise Kings: The three wise men observe the birth of a star in the East at the time of the birth of Jesus, and interpret this as the sign of the coming of the new Messiah to the Jews. The Romans have appointed King Herod to the province of Judea, and because he is concerned for his future he instructs the wise men to find the new Messiah. The wise men follow the star to Bethlehem, where they find the house and the child, and prostrate themselves before Mary and Jesus. Then they present the gifts they have brought with them: gold, frankincense and myrrh. In the frescoes one of the kings is depicted as young, one middle-aged and the third, elderly. Acknowledging that the child is indeed the new Messiah, the kings return to their countries by another route, without informing King Herod of the child's whereabouts.

Flight into Egypt: After the wise kings had returned to their homelands, angels appear to Joseph in a dream, telling him that because Herod wants to kill the infant Jesus, he must take his family and flee to Egypt and remain there for a time, as it was necessary to hide the child from the king. When Herod was unable to find Jesus, he sent his soldiers to kill all the male children in and around Bethlehem who were under two years of age. After the death of Herod, the angel appears to Joseph again to tell him that the danger is past and and that they can return to Bethlehem. In frescoes depicting the Flight into Egypt, Mary and the baby Jesus are shown riding a donkey while Joseph follows behind them.

Baptism: Jesus comes to the River Jordan to be baptized by St. John the Baptist. John protests at first, but later agrees. In this scene, John is depicted with his hand on the head of Jesus. Jesus is in the water, unclothed. Two angels extend a towel to the naked Jesus. In some of the baptism frescoes, Satan is shown muddying the waters of the river.

Raising of Lazarus From The Dead: Jesus was very fond of Martha and her brother Lazarus. Word is sent to Jesus that Lazarus has fallen ill, but when Jesus comes to see him he learns that Lazarus has been dead for four days. Jesus goes to the cave where Lazarus was buried and calls out to him, 'Lazarus, come forth'. Lazarus emerges from the grave, with cloth wrappings still on his hands and feet. The frescoes depict Lazarus wrapped in his shroud, with his siblings kneeling before him.

Transfiguration: One day Jesus takes Peter, John and James up to the mountain. They begin to pray when suddenly His face begins to change and His garments glow with a dazzling white light. At the same moment Jesus begins to speak to Moses and Elijah of His approaching death in Jerusalem, while Peter, John and James watch. The prophets are enveloped in a cloud from which a voice is heard stating that Jesus is His son and most beloved. In the Transfiguration frescoes Jesus is depicted enveloped in a shaft of light, speaking with the prophets, while Peter, John and James cower on the mountainside.

Entry into Jerusalem: As Jesus approaches Jerusalem, He sends two of his followers to go to a nearby village and purchase a donkey foal that has never been ridden and bring it to Him. As Jesus rides the donkey, those surrounding him spread their garments and branches they have gathered from the fields on the ground before him. The people of Jerusalem offer Jesus a grand welcome. In these frescoes there is a man in a tree named Zaccheus, who has not been an honest man up until that time. Zaccheus hosts Jesus in his home, and promises that henceforth he will be a good and charitable man.

The Last Supper: Seven days before the celebration of Passover, the Jews begin to eat only unleavened bread. On the first day of the holiday the meat of a sacrificial lamb is consumed at the evening meal. In the representations of the Last Supper, Jesus is depicted at the dining table surrounded by his twelve apostles. The apostle Judas has reached an agreement to deliver Jesus to the Roman soldiers in exchange for thirty pieces of silver. After the meal has been consumed, Jesus says, 'He who will betray me is among us at the table.' It is interesting that this scene is portrayed so differently in different corners of the world. In Leonardo da Vinci's painting in the Santa Maria Delle Grazie church in Milan, the apostles at the Last Supper are seated alongside one another looking in the same direction. In the cathedral in Cusco, Peru, the dish in the center of the table contains not a fish, but a Babirusa pig.

Judas's Betrayal: Jesus and His followers go the Mount of Olives to pray together, where they are met with armed soldiers and a crowd carrying sticks. Judas has agreed in advance with the soldiers that the person he kisses will be Jesus. In the Betrayal frescoes Judas is always shown in the foreground embracing Jesus, with armed soldiers in the background.

Crucifixion: At the signal from Judas, the soldiers capture Jesus and bring Him to the palace. In order to increase His suffering, a crown made of thorns is placed on the head of the red-robed Jesus. After they have finished mocking Him, they dress Him again in His own garments. As they mount the Hill of Golgotha where He is to be crucified, Jesus is made to carry His own cross. Among the crowds watching are the women who have served Jesus since Galilee, His mother Mary, and the woman named Mary Magdalene, whose identity has always been a matter of dispute in

Christianity. Jesus is nailed to the cross. In His last moments, Jesus sees his most beloved apostle, John the Evangelist, standing next to his mother, and calls out to Mary, 'Behold thy son', and to John, 'Behold thy mother'. One of the soldiers in front of Jesus pierces His breast with a spear, and another holds a sponge soaked with vinegar to His mouth. Jesus drinks the vinegar, then calls out, 'My Father, I commend My soul unto You', and dies. Two thieves have also been crucified together with Jesus. In the Crucifixion frescoes, Mary and John and, in some frescoes, the above-mentioned persons are also depicted.

CAPPADOCIA
Bilkent Kültür Girişimi Publications

Cover: The Last Supper,
Karanlık Church, Göreme,
s. 62.

Inner cover: Crucifixion,
Karanlık Church, Göreme, s.2.

Back cover: Fairy chimneys
with three caps stemming from
a single body, Zelve (Paşabağ),
s. 82

Page 4: Kızılçukur Valley.

Authors
Turgay Tuna
Bülent Demirdurak

Edited by
Gülgün Balta

Translated by
Carol LaMotte

Proofread by
Nalan Özsoy

Art direction and book design
Ersu Pekin

Editor in chief
Meltem Cansever

Artwork
Bahadır Otmanlı

Photographs
Ersin Altok
Hadiye Cangökçe
Halis Yenipınar
Hezarfen Fotoğrafya
Murat Gülyaz
Nusret Nurdan Eren
Oğuz Karakütük
Samih Rıfat
Turgay Tuna

Maps, plans and drawings
Metin Keskin

BKG-Bilkent Kültür Girişimi Publications
Yalçın Koreş Cd, Arifağa Sk, No:29
Yenibosna, Bahçelievler
İSTANBUL, TÜRKİYE
Tel: 0212 451 62 50
Faks: 0212 451 65 90
info@bkg.com.tr
Certificate number: 19167
Online sales: www.bkg.com.tr/shop/

Color separation, printing and binding
Mas Matbaacılık AŞ
Hamidiye Mah. Soğuksu Cad. 3
34408 Kağıthane-İstanbul
info@masmat.com.tr
Certificate number: 12055

ISBN: 978-605-5488-05-5
Third Edition, July 2013
© All rights reserved